THE HIDDEN JOURNEY

Melvyn Matthews is an Anglican priest currently working as Director of the Ammerdown Centre for Study and Renewal – an ecumenical, adult residential education centre near Bath.

The younger son of nonconformist parents, after reading French at Oxford University, he trained for the priesthood at King's College, London. He has been a parish priest but much of his ministry had been with students. He was a lecturer in the Department of Religious Studies in the University of Nairobi and has been on the chaplaincy team to two English universities, most recently as Senior Chaplain to Bristol University. While in Bristol he was also Vicar of the Chaplaincy Church. During his ministry he has often found himself in pioneering situations involving ecumenical teamwork and believes that the future of the Church lies in experiencing the pain and pleasure of such teams.

Melvyn Matthews is married to June, Head of Science in a church comprehensive school, and they have three childen. He enjoys politics, poetry and the cinema and is the author of *Delighting in God*, also published by Fount.

D1428312

MELVYN MATTHEWS

THE HIDDEN JOURNEY

Reflections on a Dream
by Thomas Merton

Collins
FOUNT PAPERBACKS

First published in Great Britain
by Fount Paperbacks, London in 1989

Printed and bound in Great Britain
by William Collins Sons & Co. Ltd, Glasgow

In memory of my parents
and for my children
Mark, Rachel and Simeon

ACKNOWLEDGEMENT
OF SOURCES

The author and publishers are grateful for permission to use material from R. S. Thomas, EXPERIMENTING WITH AN AMEN (Macmillan, 1986); K. Raine, COLLECTED POEMS 1935–1980 (George Allen and Unwin, 1981); and T. Merton, CONJECTURES OF A GUILTY BYSTANDER (Sheldon Press, 1977).

CONTENTS

ACKNOWLEDGEMENTS

A writer friend of mine said that he never signed contracts with his publishers because every book he wrote turned out in the end to be different from his expectations. His friendly warning came too late for this book, which has taken longer to write and has certainly turned out to be far more personal than I originally intended. It began to take shape during an expedition to the Taizé community and has been continued, off and on, in Somerset and the Lake District throughout the first year of a new job and all the upheaval which that entails. But in a way I don't regret any of this because I've had time to mull things over and let it all come out from what deeper places I've got and not just from my head – which ought to help.

I would like to thank most warmly my editor at Fount, Sarah Baird-Smith, for her amazing patience, and my wife for her encouragement (as ever!) and for the title. Some friends will inevitably recognize themselves or events in which they were involved at various points in the narrative. If I have not managed to speak to them then I would ask their indulgence in the recognition that God is at work in all of us, which is one of the things the book tries to say. Finally, the book contains so much that has come to me from my beginnings that it cannot but be offered in thankfulness to my parents. It is also for my children, with thanks, and in the hope that they will come to know – if they don't already – something of the journey of trust and hope I have tried to describe.

MELVYN MATTHEWS
Christmas 1988

1

The Inner Music

There are many books on prayer, but not all of them are about the hidden life within us. In most people's minds prayer is something which we do and, usually, ought to do more. It's regarded somewhat in the same light as physical exercise or losing weight, as "something we ought to get round to doing more of". We all think that prayer is a good thing, but cannot or will not easily bring ourselves to do it. Some of the time we need to be persuaded that it will work and that if we indulge in it we will not lose our rationality and become, somehow, over-religious; but for most of the time we regard it as something of a chore and leave it to the experts, to those who are paid to do it or who are said to be prayerful people (as if they were some special rare breed), that is to the clergy and the religious. Books or sermons about prayer quite often begin from these assumptions and so set out with the apparently laudable aim of persuading us that if only we could understand the matter correctly and do it all in the proper way, or have a stronger grip on things and work at it harder, then prayer will "work" and we will be able to "do" it – as if it were some piece of algebra or an extra hard piece of homework to which daddy or mummy has the right answers and we are only being slightly unintelligent and will soon understand.

But meanwhile the hidden life within us has remained untouched.

While reasons for prayer are helpful, particularly perhaps for those who have already embarked upon the life of prayer, they seldom persuade anybody to begin. Prayer, in the end, is not a matter of the reason and the will. The keyspring for prayer does not lie in rational persuasion or in better selling techniques by the clergy. The motivation for prayer lies much further back within the self than these conscious and deliberate activities. The motivation for prayer lies in a recognition of one's own hidden life and of prayer as the ongoing expression of it. Prayer is not something which we have to do. Prayer is happening within us. It is each person's inner music. It is already there, being uttered by the Spirit of God within each person. We don't have to do it, we have to recognize and own its occurrence.

So what is needed is not another book persuading us to do what we do not do, but a book which, like a special piece of music, will release us into prayer as a basic, continuing and necessary activity without which we know that we will die. Instead of exhortations we need to hear those tunes which echo and then re-echo within our souls and set us free to hear the music which is already being played within us by the Spirit of God. We need to have the obstacles to our inner "primary speech"[1] released, the carapace of our hardened hearts dissolved by love and sudden desire. We need to be sprung open so that the inner flood of who we really are and what we have been saying for a long time, in fact since the foundation of the universe, pours out of us again. We need to have prayer drawn out of us by desire, released from within us as our proper language. This, in the end, is the more permanent solution, rather than seeing prayer as an activity about which we have to be rationally convinced before we can set about it; as if reading a book of rules about football could provide us with the ability to play the game.

The pity of it is that nothing much happens like that within the more formal structures of religion. Religious structures are themselves pieces of music but we treat them (and so they treat us) as if they were set pieces for an examination, only to be played in a precise way known to the examiner, rather than melodies capable of infinite variation and able to appeal to each age afresh. Novelists and poets, I find, are much more in tune with people's inner music than theologians, as are many who deal with the inner life. Consequently I think those of us in the business of religion should listen far more closely to what these novelists, poets and counsellors are saying about what is going on within people than, traditionally at least, we have done. We might then be more suprised by grace than we at least give the impression of being stuck in our lonely pulpits.

This book is an attempt to provide us with one such piece of music, which, as it is read and heard, will draw out of us prayer and consciousness of the divine life within. After a long meditation on the whole question of the "inner" life, sparked off by a visit I once made to an elderly parishioner, the book takes the form of a series of extended reflections on themes suggested by a dream recounted by Thomas Merton. This occurs at the beginning of his book *Conjectures of a Guilty Bystander.*[2] In this dream he is invited to a party but cannot reach it until he decides to swim to the further shore where he is met by the child with the white bread. The elements of the dream are understood to be symbolic of some of the central elements of the hidden life which all of us have within us but cannot or do not always see or know about. We have to see and own them in order to become ourselves. The dream is reproduced immediately after this introduction, but I would like it to be prefaced, as it were, by a serious health warning. This is because I am very sensible of the power of Thomas Merton's thinking and of how that thinking – as with that of any powerful religious thinker – can replace our own and so prevent us from having confidence in the life of God in each one of us. The dream is Merton's, not ours. The object of recalling it is not to persuade us to have the same dream but to prompt us to do our own dreaming. The object is to enable the reader to see, have confidence in and own what has been going on within him or her anyway, and so to release an awareness of the working of God and a glad acceptance of the spiritual life. Each one of us has this journey to make. It is true to say that the journey is already taking place, hidden, within us. We are already embarked. The question is whether we will make it our own and so live, or continually try to exist as if the journey were not there, or live as if it was always somewhere else and we had to find it, or even as if we always had to swim against or across the tide. The aim of this book is to invoke in people the desire to pray, to swim, to join in the music or, rather, to allow the music of God to play in them.

The Dream

I am invited to a party. The people are dressed in fine new clothes, walking about by the waterfront of a small fishing village of old stone houses. The gay, light dresses of the women contrast with the dark stones of the houses. I am invited to the party with them, and suddenly they are all gone, and the party is much further away than I thought it would be. I must get there in a boat. I am all alone; the boat is at the quay.

A man of the town says that for five dollars I can get across on a yacht. I have five dollars, more than five dollars, hundreds of dollars, and also francs. He takes me to the yacht, but it is not a yacht. It is a workaday fishing schooner, which I prefer. But it does not move from shore. It is very heavy. We try to push it off, it does not move, we try in many ways to make it move, and it seems to have moved a little. But then I know that I must strike out and swim.

And I am swimming ahead in the beautiful magic water of the bay. From the clear depths of the water comes a wonderful life to which I am not entitled, a life and a power which I both love and fear. I know that by diving down into the water I can find wonders and joys, but that it is not for me to dive down; rather I must go to the other side. The other side is there. The end of the swim. The house is on the shore. The wide summer house which I am reaching with the strength which came to me from the water. The water is great and vast beneath me as I come toward the shore. And I have arrived. I am out of the water. I know now all that I must do in the summer house. I know that I must first play with this dog who comes running from one of the halls.

I know the Child will come, and He comes. The Child comes and smiles. It is the smile of a Great One, hidden. He gives to me, in simplicity, two pieces of buttered white bread, the ritual and hieratic meal given to all who come to stay.

The Hidden Journey

I once visited an elderly lady who was in hospital. While I was sitting with her the conversation drifted in and out of the past. At one moment we were talking about that particular day, what had happened, who had visited her, what the doctors were doing and so on. At the next moment, without anything being said to mark the transition, we were talking about a day in her well-stored past, and I was being told about a tennis match which she had just played with her brothers. Part of the time that afternoon I was in a hospital ward, part of the time I was watching tennis on another summer afternoon some considerable time ago. Not, I fancy, an uncommon experience for anyone who regularly visits the elderly. I was later asked by the lady's friends how she was and recounted the incident. "Ah yes," somebody said, "she's got a very strong *inner life.*"

Most of the time this inner life is quite dormant, but this incident showed me that it is actually very real, and not so "inner" as I thought. In fact my friend's so-called inner life kept bursting out, and insisted on mingling with what I had assumed was reality. I came away from the hospital thinking that our inner life is hardly, properly speaking, an "inner" life at all, and if we talk about an inner life then we should not imply that this is a reality which is quite distinct and separate from our everyday lives. The inner life is not a separate entity. My visit to that elderly lady had provided me with very sharp evidence that what her friend called her inner life – in fact her past memories – was just, indeed hardly, below the surface. It only required a few days in hospital, where the tensions and preoccupations of getting dressed and finding meals were taken away, for this apparently inner life to become her outer clothing. It was actually very much nearer the surface than she knew or I expected!

Then I thought that she was no exception. What was true for her was also true for the rest of us. What we call the inner life is much nearer to us than we know and we live by it more than we know. It breaks into the stream of our immediate consciousness more than we would like to believe. In the case of my elderly lady it was fairly clear, at least to me, when we were in the hospital and when we were playing tennis. She did not notice the transition, and that, I thought, is how it is in reality; that is what is happening to all of us all of the time. Our inner life breaks into the surface of our existence at every point but we are hardly conscious of it happening. Yet if we have read even a little modern psychology then we should know that it is this inner life that helps us order our perceptions, shape our understanding, receive what we see and hear and how we should see and hear it. Indeed there is no final distinction between the outer and the inner life. What our past has been, what our predominant memories and former assumptions are, how those things have affected and continue to affect us, how we have assimilated our joys and sorrows, all this governs very largely how we perceive and value what is happening to us now. There are even some things which happen to us in the present which we do not see or hear because of what we have allowed our past to make of us. A literary example of this is to be found in the novel by E. M. Forster, *A Passage to India*, where Dr Aziz is not "seen" by the ladies at the Residence and they drive off in his carriage. He was, after all, an Indian and for the purpose of riding in carriages he was not there. Such incidents can be repeated daily in everyday life and are the regular experience of women, of blacks and of the disabled.

So I came to the conclusion that human beings do not really consist of two parts, one being the inner life, associated with dreams or psychiatrists' couches or, perhaps, religion, and the other being the outer shell of everyday historical living – work, shopping, marriage, action and the like. These two merge into each other. Unfortunately, however, popular mythology does not make this distinction. In this popular view human beings are rather like tinned goods with coloured labels denoting who they are and what they are for, but inside they have a completely separate existence which may or may not be healthy. In popular understanding this interior existence is accessed by dreams or by analysis, but it is usually completely out of reach and normally should remain so. We only need to know about it when it goes bad and threatens to invade or disrupt our everyday existence. At that point a psychiatrist is called in to put it right and to allow us to carry on as before. It is as if we were carrying around inside us a sort of black bag, the repository of all that we do not want or need or understand. This black bag is normally kept firmly shut and unopened.

A further reflection after my hospital visit was that people and even societies – groups of people – often quite unwittingly employ a number of different mechanisms as means of keeping this little black bag shut. Two of the most popular are religion and education. For it is often said that the purpose of education or religion is to enable us to lead the good life or the moral life. But a little thought will show that when we say "good" or "moral" we very often mean "controlled". What we are really trying to do is to control that which we fear will get out of control. The fear is that if we let the ingredients of the bag loose then life as we know it will become uncontainable. This popular way of seeing things is often encouraged and effectively reinforced by those who are or who wish to be in control in society. For them the most important thing is the preservation of order. Although it may well be denied, education and religion quite easily and quickly become the forces which those in power try to use to preserve order and to contain the uncontainable. Human beings, it is said, are inherently sinful and need religion (or, if the speaker is not a believer, education) to keep themselves from falling. It was this way of understanding religion that caused Karl Marx to condemn all of it as being no more than a means of keeping the powerful where they are. For him this demonstrated how corrupt religious systems were. His view was too sweeping, but with greater psychological insight than was perhaps available to Marx we can now see that if we do use religion or education in this way then we are projecting onto the social level something that is happening within ourselves. We have convinced ourselves by various means that living is a matter of keeping potentially divisive internal forces, whether personal or social, under strict control. It is about keeping your little black bag shut.

All this, of course, reduces education and religion to being means to a particular end. It also reveals that we think that the areas of our existence that we know nothing about are automatically bad or "black". It ignores the reality of education and religion as ends in themselves, as true expressions within their own terms of beauty and the quest for truth. It is a way of behaving that uses what are essentially good things as means of control under the fear that there is, somewhere within us, a little black bag which has to be kept firmly shut. It is not a question of denying that evil exists – how could we doubt that – but of trying to analyse how the forces of evil operate, of trying to work out how they actually get hold of us. Evil forces actually operate, I think, in a quite different way. They swing into force to provoke us into an over-reaction when we are criticized. Evil forces foster our assumptions of grandeur and tell us, when we are in power, that we have the God-given task of keeping the dark forces within humanity at bay.

If all this sounds absurdly overstated then we only have to look back a generation and see that this pattern was very clearly at work within Hitler's Germany. A moment's thought will show that it is also at work in a number of other countries today. In pre-war Germany various areas of life, in particular the Jewish area, were identified as dark, and subdued or eliminated, because they were said to be opposed to the forces of light, law and order represented by Aryan purity. The Church was drafted in to support these policies and church leaders appointed who accepted that the role of the Church in the state was as the state defined it. In accordance with this policy those with Jewish ancestry were barred from holding office in the Church. So the German Church struggle began of which Dietrich Bonhoeffer is a representative martyr. A similar pattern of events is not so very far away from any one of us as soon as we accept that there is, within each individual, an area which is separate, unknown and potentially unknowable, and which must be controlled by the human will because it is assumed to be evil. The roots of political fascism lie within a view of human nature which sees it as essentially divided against itself.

Very few contemporary theologians have seen this process at work in society and commented upon it from a theological point of view. Nikolai Berdyayev was one. In modern times, Rowan Williams has written about it in his book *The Truce of God*. He discusses the nature of violence in society and in particular the fantasies about violence which our current interests in space fiction and so on reveal. He says that the popular view is that violence "happens" to us. We think we are invaded somehow by forces over which we have no control. If we look at the popular press or the cinema or the literature which so many people read or the videos which they watch, then we will soon see how permeated all these things are by a mentality which divides things into light and darkness and in which the darkness is evil and uncontrollable, about to invade the light at any minute and for no foreseeable reason. Professor Williams calls for us to abandon this view and to be converted to responsible living. We have to relearn our original dignity and deny that nothing can be done. It is, really, this moral maturity that we have lost. This maturity is based upon a positive hope, a denial that everything has to be done by control, and a realization that we can actually choose the good. The Gospel sets us free from fantasy and also sets us free to live in one world which is God's and in which he calls us to be his children.

I know that all this is a long way from my little old lady in hospital, but my reflections upon that incident have led me to see that we often try to divide ourselves into two. I also came to see that personally and socially this is a disaster. Personally it is a disaster because it leads to a lack of self-love. Socially it is a disaster because it provides the seedbed for repression. I now believe that human beings do not really work by dividing themselves into two parts, one being the inner life, accessed through psychiatric means, the other being the outer, regular, historical existence of every-day events. These two, apparently separate, worlds are in fact one and gloriously so. We might make a practical distinction between our inner life, calling it settled or disturbed or whatever we feel it is, and our outer everyday life, saying that it has been busy or peaceful or whatever; but this can only be a conven-ience of speech and not something which reflects a whole philosophy of life. If we erect this convenience of speech into a philosophy then we shall be guilty of projecting our sense of inner schism on to reality and dividing that reality into dark and light, good and bad. As we have already seen history should teach us at this point that such projections are not innocent, but result in the most disastrous social divisions that mankind has experienced. Such a philosophy also destroys our hope and leads us to the need to exercise control over reality as if that reality were either our own or something totally alien and fearsome.

Such a view also leads to a distorted view of religion. It is particularly disastrous if religious people magnify this distinction of convenience and come to believe not only that there is an inner life as distinct from an outer one but that it is this inner life which carries our religious awareness. We cannot imply that awareness of God is solely an inner activity without risking the implication that we must forget or put away our real lives in order to enter the realm of God's existence or activity. I think it is true that for many people today these "outer" areas of life are somehow not able to carry religious awareness in the same way that perhaps they used to do. People feel that historical existence is not necessarily bad or evil in itself, but it has become detached somehow from the main stream of religious awareness. Religious awareness is now a very personal, private and interior matter. It has become almost completely a matter of private and personal experience. At best the outer life is neutral. Those who believe this may even further capitalize on this artificial distinction by turning the whole thing on its head and claim that the "inner" life is the only "real" life. If this is the case then everything that happens to us in the outside world should be ignored or forgotten, or even dismissed as an illusion before we can lead the truly spiritual life which God wants us to lead. This is extremely convenient for so-called religious people when the events of this real world are very uncomfortable, potentially disastrous and seemingly impossible to resolve.

As we shall see, our everyday existence *is* subject to illusion and it is the primary task of Christian people to free themselves from that illusion so that they can see themselves as they are seen and the world as it truly is. But the world itself, the everyday, historical world in which we have our existence, is not, of itself, illusory. It is gift, and what is more it is gift from God. Because it is gift it is real and it is unitary. We are given it all at once. What we cannot do is see it all at once because we are limited and finite beings. But that does not mean to say that it is actually divided in any way. The limitations of sight and the need of human beings for mercy and forgiveness are not, in themselves, indications that the world we live in is somehow unreal. Only our perception of it is foreshortened. Whatever we do we cannot accept either of the popular misconceptions that will present themselves to us in our day. One is that the inner life is the better life, that it is a totally separate area of our existence where true values prevail and where God exists. The other is that the material, historical world is the only world and that all talk of a life of the spirit is meaningless and since the advent of science, disproven.

My old lady demonstrated that such distinctions are not supported by human experience. Nor are they part of Christian understanding. Christians do not believe that there are two worlds and that the inner world exists apart from the world of action, fact and history. Just as much popular psychiatry implies that there are two worlds, one external and good and the other interior and at least potentially if not actually rotten, the home of Oedipus complexes, penis envies and the like, so much popular Christianity still suffers from the implicit assumption that there is a material world, which is real, and another world, concerned with values or goodness and truth, which is accessed by prayer and worship. But the traditional Christian affirmation, much lost in the present climate of western civilization, and which my friend in hospital brought me back to, is that there is only one world which is both good and real. We live with our past and our present together. We live with our inner and outer lives together. What we think of as the good and what we think of as the real are not separate. The essence of the Christian doctrine of creation is an affirmation of the unity, reality and goodness of all things. The universe is a unity and this unity is both good and real because it derives its being from God who is one, good and the source of all reality. There is no inner or outer side to all that is. There are just things that we human beings cannot see.

Talk about an inner life then, or the "interior life" as it is often called, risks reinforcing popular misunderstandings of how things are on at least two counts. It is alien to the way human beings actually work and it also undermines the Christian affirmation in the unity, goodness and reality of the creation. But at this point people will object that there is a form of separation, or at least a split involved in living. We sense, often very sharply, that we are not unified beings, not at one with ourselves or the world in which we live. How then are we to understand that sense of disunity? We should not underestimate it. My pastoral experience is that this sense of disunity within human beings is very acute. People often speak of their sense of distance from reality, their inability to relate to others, their feeling of being apart from things, dislocated in some way. My faith has been, and I think that the faith of the Church is exactly this, that in spite of our sense of dislocation there is no permanent or real distance between ourselves and reality. We may well have become separate from things by the actions of others, by our own actions, or by the state of the society in which we live, but this cannot be given the dignity of being the final reality. Our sense of angst is real enough as experience but is no indication of the true state of affairs. It is not "how things are". Our sense of dislocation is often sharpened by our sense of choice and the importance our modern age places upon individual choices, but we ought to be totally unsure as to whether reality is some sort of package which we can choose – with great blowings of philosophical trumpets about the value and dignity of human choice – or reject just like that. We cannot do either. Reality is part of us already. From the beginning we are part of "how things are" and happiness consists in accepting and owning that this is the case. Reality is one and we are part of that reality. We do not float above it, able to choose whether we are to belong to it or able to choose which parts of it we shall belong to as if we were supra-real beings. Various questions then arise in our minds. How does this deep sense of disunity arise? If it is so unreal why does it persist and why can we not see it to be unreal? Why can't we see things as they really are? Human beings, as they are understood within the Christian tradition, cannot see "how things are" because they allow themselves to be governed and controlled by a particular set of imperatives. We experience ourselves as being split, often with intense pain, because we are governed by external forces. These forces are imperative and very demanding and it is only occasionally, very occasionally, that human beings are given the possibility of experiencing things as a single unity. When such experiences come they are very intense, known to be the truth about how things are, and deeply formative; but for the most part, in fact normally, we are kept from them by the imperious nature of those forces which bind us to themselves. In 1985 Michael Mayne, who was then Vicar of the University Church in Cambridge and is now Dean of Westminster, was stricken with a very severe but mysterious illness. He became extremely weak, unable to walk and suffered great pain. Eventually the disease was diagnosed as benign Myalgic Encephalomyelitis. Mayne went through a long process of personal reassessment because of this illness and eventually asked one of his counsellors, a professional psychiatrist, why it was that he had become so ill. Why was his resistance to this particular virus so low? He was given a very interesting and testing reply. "Perhaps," he said, with a smile, "because your inscape does not match your landscape." Mayne had been living a very split existence – a common but often unnoticed disease amongst clergy. He was living in a state where his true self and his false self were unreconciled. The strain was such that in the end his bodily resistances were so reduced that he contracted this virus. Mayne wrote a book about the whole event afterwards. In it he says, "This gap between 'inscape' and 'landscape' is true of all of us, but it is a particular temptation of the professional, the public person: and I guess it may be a particular failure of the clergy. It leads to temptation and guilt, very often unacknow-ledged, which can leave you drained and vulnerable."[1] This event, recorded by a brave and honest man able to articulate his experience and share it with others in a very public manner, can only be the tip of the iceberg of what is happening to so many others vastly less able to understand and articulate what is happening to them, let alone able to have the time off and the professional care that Mayne received. This is not to be in the least bit critical, but simply to point out that if this is what is happening to one man in that position a great deal more must be happening to so many others. We are in the grip of powerful imperatives which tear us away from our inscape.

These imperatives, once adopted, regulate how we see things. We have a set, indeed at least one set, of these imperatives in each generation and in each coun-try. These imperatives can be personal and individual, as in the case of Michael Mayne, or they can be socially generated and experienced. Those which are socially generated usually take a benevolent form such as "Democracy" or "Parliamentary Rule", but they may become divisive or demonic such as "Apartheid" or even "Individual Choice", "Social Progress" or "Suc-cess". In theological or philosophical language these socially-generated imperatives can become hyposta-tized or absolutized. We tend very easily, especially in periods of social change or malaise, to give these imperatives a very unreal identity and then say that we cannot live, indeed must not live, by anything else.

Even the most benevolent and initially useful imperatives can, in this way, assume a demonic form. One of these is "Material Progress". Initially this is a necessary concept of social health and cohesion, but when absolutized it becomes a means of social domination, both over those who are subject to it and over those who wish to use it for their own ends. In this way we create our own alienations. We are in fact self-alienating beings.

In the Christian spiritual tradition, salvation really means discovering that this is what we have done and then allowing that discovery to set us free from the power that these imperatives exert over us. We then see that reality is one, that there is no divide between ourselves and reality, and no divide between an inner spiritual realm of goodness and an outer shell of history and fact. To affirm the unity of reality is to affirm belief in God. When this unity is affirmed people say that they can "see". They are seeing things with the eye of the divine. God is the invisible and hidden ground of love for all creation, the hidden ground of the unity of all things. Faith in this hidden ground of love replaces faith in the authority of all other powers. It dispenses with the need to place our trust in anything else. This need, this irrational surd in our consciousness, to place our confidence in something else, something visible, tangible and apparently beneficent, is the source of our contemporary dislocation. Trust in what is hidden, on the other hand, places us within the clear ground of confidence in the unseen, which is the love of God. It enables us to see the unseen. It is within this love that, if we would but accept it, we have existed from the beginning. We need nothing else.

Trust in the unseen love of God is that which frees and unifies the human spirit. It frees us from the need to trust other things as the source of salvation. It unifies because it is, in itself, an affirmation of the unity of creation and of the self as part of that creation. It sends fleeing all the dark shadows of the night and renews the self as loved and enlightened from the beginning. It recognizes that what we feared as realities – imperious realities which we have to obey – are no more than the shadows cast upon the ground by the strength of the light in which we stand.

The importance of these experiences of trust in the unseen has long been known to poets. Wordsworth is probably the English poet who speaks of them most clearly. His poetry records his awareness of an unseen Presence. He also knows that this dark, inscrutable Presence, if trusted and acknowledged rather than feared and disowned, works a healing in the soul. He is similarly aware of the need for solitude so that this Presence may be allowed to do its work within us. The fact that Wordsworth's trust in the unseen is couched in the language of nineteenth-century romanticism and its concomitant reverence for nature should be no detraction. Awareness of the unseen Presence and of the necessity of trust in this Presence is, time and time again in the history of Christian thinking, linked to an awareness of the beauty and healing power of the created world. The important point is that Wordsworth had learned to trust in the unseen.

Dust as we are, the immortal spirit grows
Like harmony in music; there is a dark

Inscrutable workmanship that reconciles
Discordant elements, makes them cling together
In one society.[2]

A voice less sentimental than that of Wordsworth is the twentieth-century Welsh poet, R. S. Thomas. He knows and writes clearly of the need to be aware of and trust in the unseen in the face of the doubt and despair of the modern age. Thomas is deeply aware of the threat not of the unseen but of the seen, of the machine of civilization which threatens to extinguish our capacity for allowing the "Inscrutable workmanship" to perform its task in us. His poetry is sharper and more honest about the human person but perhaps because of that more impressive in the way it asks us to thrust our hand into the dark hole in the side of Christ. It is poetry which is aware of the infinite silence of God, which compares the salvation of the soul to the slow growth of lichen upon stone, which sees prayers as no more than:

> . . . gravel
> flung at the sky's
> window, hoping to attract
> the loved one's attention

but which does not stop because,

> . . . peering once
> through my locked fingers
> I thought that I detected
> the movement of a curtain.[3]

Yet this necessity, the capacity for trust in the unseen God, is at a great premium in Western society.

Health is found, it is assumed, in what can be seen or measured. Nor should we be easily persuaded that the current interest in health by means of personal relationships is any more than a further manifestation of this materialism. We are at present deeply preoccupied by the need for personal relationships. Health and happiness for the individual is assumed to come if not only then at least largely through these relationships. Being solitary is regarded as a form of loss, an escape from human company. Getting it right with people is primary.

But it should have occurred to us by now that such a view is severely circumscribed. In reality large sections of society, as well as enormous numbers of individuals, actually actively seek silence and solitude. This may be for apparently secular reasons, such as the pursuit of angling or walking, or it may be for openly religious reasons such as making a retreat, but so many more people than popular conceptions allow actually live with solitude as part of their everyday existence. They may be old or they may be single, for not everybody lives in a family. In reality it is only a small proportion of people in the Western nations who live with others all of the time, and those who do find the need to get away from it all. Moreover it is now becoming clear that neither the New Testament nor the findings of human psychology give support to the view that health or salvation can only come when our personal relationships are all close, profound and fully integrated.

The New Testament speaks of the Church, but this is a belonging "in Christ". Christ is the focus of the ecclesial body. Belonging to that ecclesial body certainly carries with it certain duties towards the other members of it, but the New Testament does not regard the fulfilling of those other ecclesial duties as being in itself salvific. Belonging to the Church is not an end in itself. That belonging comes about as a result of the person's relationship with Christ. It may be required by that relationship but it is that relationship – embodied in an acceptance of death and resurrection as being the way of truth – which is central and primary.

Meanwhile there are a number of question marks being raised, by those who work in the field of human psychology, against the view that intimate personal relationships are the only, or at least the primary, means of happiness and salvation. The first comes from those who have seen that much of the present vogue for psychotherapy is fundamentally conservative in its approach, doing no more than restoring the sick or disturbed person to his or her place in the society which has been the very cause of the disturbance. Kenneth Leech makes this point when he asks, "What are therapy and counselling actually doing about the problems confronting human society? Are they in fact simply helping people to be well adjusted in a society whose fundamental values and interests remain unquestioned?"[4] But the clearest voice comes from Anthony Storr, who in his recent book *The School of Genius*, makes it abundantly clear that solitude is as much the source of genuine creativity as personal relationships. Desire for solitude – as Christians should have known from the example of Christ – is not aberrant behaviour; rather it is a potent source

of restructuring both for the interior life of the individual and for the communal life of the society of which
he is a part. Storr writes, "The current emphasis upon
intimate personal relationships as the touchstone of
health and happiness is a comparatively recent
phenomenon. Earlier generations would not have rated
human relationships so highly . . ." He goes on to
point out that this modern view of the importance of
intimate personal relationships has the consequence of
raising sexual relationships to a level of value which
they were not designed to carry. Marriage, also, comes
to bear a burden of value and expectancy which it
cannot support, at least while it is defined in the terms
normalized in Western society. The health of the
human person needs solitude in order to grow, and
grows as much in loss as in success. "It appears,
therefore, that some development of the capacity to be
alone is necessary if the brain is to function at its best
and if the individual is to fulfil his highest potential.
Human beings easily become alienated from their own
deepest needs and feelings. Learning, thinking, inno-
vation and maintaining contact with one's own inner
world are all facilitated by solitude."[5]

There are numerous examples of how true all this is.
One of the most impressive of the many quoted by
Storr is that of Admiral Byrd, who had to man an
advanced weather station in the Antarctic in 1934. He
insisted on being alone, because his life – which was
outwardly happy and fulfilled – had reached the stage
of seeming confused and crowded. His diary records
how in the solitude he felt "more alive" than at any
other time in his life. He knew his despair to be
groundless and his disunity to be apparent. He was

part of a single cosmos. Western society makes the realization of this unity extremely difficult. There is the constant presence of the media, of noise, of meaningless music in shopping malls. There is the ubiquitous television screen, often in serried ranks as if one or two were not enough. There is the car telephone and the portable stereo. None of these are in themselves in any way evil or immoral. What is difficult to understand is the drive which makes them necessary to us. We seem unable to be alone. Perhaps merely because it is possible we think we need continuous contact with what we assume to be "the world". And yet, as we have already discovered, there is pressing evidence that large numbers of people actually do seek solitude. Angling, an essentially solitary sport, is one of the most popular in Britain. Constantly brave individuals decide to cross the Atlantic or the Sahara Desert on their own. More and more people, some believers, as many not, seek the silence of our retreat houses. Nor does the monastic vocation show any sign of actually disappearing in the modern world. Trust in the unseen is understood by many to be life-giving.

Anthony Storr's own interpretation of this phenomenon is severely psychological, seeing solitude as an integrating force for the human personality – and we should be profoundly grateful for this contemporary restatement of such a necessity. But at several points in his argument Storr carefully dissociates himself from those who, like Wordsworth or Traherne, would find an explicit transcendental reference in this need. Not so careful is Thomas Merton. Merton wrote a great deal about solitude, both for the sake of those who had already embraced it as a vocation but also for those who could see it as no more than an encumbrance in the pursuit of peace and justice in the world. He makes a number of important and often forgotten points. One of the most important is that solitude is not negative. It is, rather, a quest for unity. Nor is the solitude simply his, something which feeds and belongs to the solitary alone. The solitary unites himself with others, albeit at a deeper, mystical level. Above all it is an embarkation upon a struggle to be free of illusion, of illusion about the importance of the self, of illusion about the need to produce, of illusion about this world. It is not an escape from this world but a protest against the illusory power of this world by turning to the love of God alone. Rather than being an escape it is a reaffirmation of what the world really is, it is an attempt to hold things together as they are in truth. For the love of God is found to be a unitive love, not a love for the individual soul alone but a love which unites that soul to itself, to creation and to all other beings, for it is the ground of being itself. Merton says, "The contemplative has nothing to tell you except to reassure you and to say that if you dare penetrate your own silence and dare to advance without fear into the silence of your own heart, and risk the sharing of that solitude with the lonely other who seeks God through you and with you, then you will truly recover the light and the capacity to understand what is beyond words and beyond explanations because it is too close to be explained: it is the intimate union in the depths of your own heart, of God's spirit and your own secret inmost self."[6]

The other point which Merton constantly makes – and made during his lifetime by practical dialogue with such figures as the Berrigan brothers and Rosemary Radford Reuther – is that the option for solitude is a political statement. He says clearly, "If a solitary should one day find his way, by the grace and mercy of God, into a desert place ... he may perhaps do more good to the human race by being a solitary than he ever could have done by remaining the prisoner of the society where he was living. For anyone who breaks the chains of falsity, and strives, even unsuccessfully, to be true to God and to his inner self, is doing more for the world than can be done even by a saint in politics ..."[7] What Merton meant by this has two aspects to it. He meant that the contemplative person cannot in any way be divorced from the political setting in which he does his contemplation. Simply by making that choice he or she is asserting that the political forces which are producing the kind of world in which we live need not operate as they do. They are not sovereign. By cutting yourself away from their power you are asserting the possibility of an entirely different sort of world. This type of insight understands prayer as an essentially subversive activity, one which by its very existence undermines the fixity of political choices. The other thing that Merton is saying in this statement is that the politician requires the contemplative in order to be a politician. In order to be effective, politics must take into account the nature of the human person. Human beings are naturally contemplative and not simply machines with certain material needs which the pursuit of politics answers. Mature religion as well as mature politics requires solitude. Indeed both Merton and Storr would say that maturity itself is generated within and requires solitude. A generation before Anthony Storr, Merton had written, "Without solitude of some sort there is and can be no maturity."[8] Merton then goes on to deepen that insight by saying that the innermost self which solitude releases is, in the end, not mine. It *is*, and by being itself it is Christ, dwelling in me.

But the essential nature of solitude is little understood and much resisted, even in intelligent Christian circles. We feel too much that we are called to be a servant Church involved in the world. We feel too much that doctrine matters. We feel too much that Church structures need to be reformed. Servanthood, doctrine and Church structures are all important, but when seen as solely important they themselves become a form of materialism and their pursuit becomes a form of enslavement. The Christian life, under the guise of being apostolic, is often deeply embroiled in the activist spirit of the age and so less able to see the face of God than it thinks. This was brought home to me a few years ago when I was involved in the preparation and presentation of a series of lenten discussion groups for an ecumenical group of churches. We proposed a number of subjects which included discussion of themes focusing around the experience of Jesus in Gethsemane and Golgotha. We asked people to talk about things like suffering, sacrifice, success and solitude. At the meeting afterwards when the groups reported on how things had gone it was very clear that the one subject which they had found most difficult to understand was solitude. They could not accept that this had any real importance for them. It grated on their social and religious consciousness. I thought afterwards what a great sadness it was that some of the most clever and articulate people from some of the most successful and active churches in that particular city had been unable to understand something of the necessity of solitude even in the face of Christ's example. But then I looked at the situation again. Was it *because* they were members of socially active and articulate churches that they were unable to understand this necessity? Was it *because* they were all members of churches which were busy preventing people from being alone and had defined this as a God-given task that they were unable to see that solitude itself might be salvific? The Christian life had already been defined for them in terms which excluded that category – solitude – and its accompaniment – silence – as being in any way God-bearing.

But while middle-class Christians reject solitude I rejoice to find that so many others, often without any explicit or dogmatic religious allegiance, keep the witness alive. The number of those deliberately seeking solitude as hermits has risen sharply in recent years right across Europe. Monasteries and convents report increased requests from those seeking solitude or silence, often from those whose life style or profession is frenetic or filled with risk. The retreat movement is booming. People may well have mixed motives, but they often see that a change of heart is required, that the Gospel does call us to a more profound and biblical faithfulness, and that the sort of society we have – and the churches which support that society – is no place where this change of heart can take place in any depth. They know that they need to learn to trust the invisible.

The consequences of all this are manifold and the

pages which follow will attempt to spell some of them out, but there are two consequences which are of particular importance and which we need to understand from the outset.

The first is that Christians should be careful before they speak of the "spiritual" life. The second is that they should not speak. Let me explain what I mean. The word "spiritual" has become obsolete for theologians. Like so many other words which were originally of immense importance to the articulation of the Christian Gospel, such as "freedom" – which has been highjacked by the present age to mean "individual choice" – the word "spiritual" has taken on a secular meaning. It is now associated with the so-called spirit world and usually means something like "ethereal" or "ghostly". It implies a sense of division between this world and another. So it might well be better, in view of everything that we have said so far, if instead of talking about the "spiritual" life or the "inner" life, we talked instead about the "hidden" life. To be a spiritual person is not to be someone who develops his or her own inner muscles, but to be someone who is perceptive of hidden realities. He or she is someone who sees and trusts the unseen. This might well necessitate, indeed should necessitate, a greater awareness of everything within one's own spirit that denies or prevents goodness within ourselves and the perception of goodness in others; but this is based upon or derives from the ability to perceive hidden realities in our lives and in the life of society. And we can only do this when we are looking towards God, because in his light what is true shines and what is untrue becomes tawdry and unreal. The light of God shows up what is hidden and

41

its reality or otherwise becomes apparent; but that can only be done when the perceiver looks towards God first and then sees all things in the light of that perception. Spiritual realities are not ethereal realities, somehow unreal or ghostly compared to "this" world, but *hidden* realities – things, truths, ways of being, which for the moment we cannot see clearly, but which, for our health's sake, we need to see.

Apply this for a moment to my hospital visit. It was my parishioner's hidden life which suddenly came to the fore. It was, as I was gradually becoming aware in my understanding of her, her relationship with her two brothers, both powerful and interesting men, which coloured so much of what she was and had always been. Anybody who cared for her had to understand that from the beginning before the care they offered could be effective. The tennis match with these brothers was always present, but hidden. If I, as her pastor, spent so much time developing my religious experience or enjoying my capacity to speak in tongues (which I don't have!) that I was unable to see that hidden tennis match within the life of this friend then I could not be said to be a spiritual person at all. The practice of spirituality is the practice of seeing things as they really are, deprived of their covering. Being a spiritual person means being able to perceive, for example, how things like tennis matches affect people, how potentially good things have become illusory imperatives we think we need in order to live. It means seeing that these imperatives are just that, illusory and divisive, while the true values which we as God's children have within us are so often forgotten, covered over by our desperate desire for identity, hidden by

what theologians have always called sin. What we need
to have is the confidence to rediscover what we as
human beings have been given from the beginning –
which is love as the hidden ground of our being.

In my hospital visit these hidden realities had been
forcibly uncovered by hospital life and sickness. This
often occurs. Sometimes it so frightens people that
they have to "recover"; the use of this very word, "recover", clearly gives the game away. When we get
better we so very often come back to a condition in
which the hidden realities have once again been covered over and hidden from view. But these moments
in hospital when our tennis matches (and we all have
the equivalent) come to the fore are extremely precious. They are moments of unity, when our illusions
fall away, when our fear of the unknown side of
ourselves is lost, and we stand face to face with God in
our entirety.

The second consequence is that we should not speak.
We need, for our health's sake first of all, but above all
for the sake of a greater awareness of the glory and
beauty of God, to remain more silent. The life of faith,
in word and work as well as in worship, must carry
within it the silence of adoration. This is not the silence
of ignorance, nor the silence of exhaustion in the quest
to find the right words, but the silence of adoration in
the face of total beauty. Our worship needs to burst
with this silence and to be swept clean of so much
unnecessary verbiage. We cannot be expected, as our
liturgical committees seem to expect, to carry within
our psyches the whole of the Christian credal tradition
and all its complexities in order to express our delight
in God. Our worship is overweighted, as if with the

fear that unless all is included (at least as an alternative) then something is not said. Delight in God has to spring up afresh in every heart and in every generation. Space has to be created for that expression to germinate. Too many words stifle delight. In the worship of the ecumenical community of Taizé in France, simplicity of verbal expression is accompanied by long, deep silences, sometimes as long as ten or more minutes, during the common prayer. Worship there has the effect of allowing the person to become aware of the hidden Christ within by removing all obstacles to that awareness except the bare minimum required by the Christian tradition – a psalm, two or three verses of scripture and a few, simple hymn chants all connected by long silences. This increasingly has to be our path. Only such silence will enable us to come to terms with the grandeur and beauty of God. Only such silence will allow us to adore him in his reality rather than the reality we have created for him. Our problem, I think, derives from the adoption by the modern consciousness of a reductionist understanding of knowledge. We assume that because the Christian tradition has spoken so often about God that we know all that it is necessary to know about him, provided we can set this knowing down in a clear enough fashion. We think that this is enough – all we need to do. Then, when we don't know we can turn to those who do to tell us what has been set down. This, apparently, will then restore our confidence in the fact that God exists. We do not, it seems, need to become aware, we simply need to know and to know in such a way that we can write it down. This turns Christian living and Christian worship into a very dubious form of education. But Christian living and Christian worship cannot be reduced to the following of primitive sets of instructions. They are, primarily, means of entry into awareness of the transcendent and awareness of the reality of the transcendent now, where we are. It has been well said that we know as much about God as one person can see of an ocean standing beside it on a dark night with a lighted candle in their hand. We desperately need, within the Christian churches, to recover that sense of standing beside this dark sea, trusting it in spite of its awesomeness, and being washed and cleansed by its beauty and its depth. In the end only the silence of adoration will allow us to do that and only then if, in the silence, we attend to what, or rather who, it contains.

So who we are as human beings lies hidden deep within us. It is, in the final analysis, only love and so has been rightly called, "the hidden ground of love"[9] We become true human beings, truly faithful and believing human beings, when we accept that the ground of our being is the mystery of love, and trust that those with whom we are engaged, namely our neighbours, also have love as the ground of their being. Our trust in ourselves and in them should – although experience shows that it may not – call out love from within them as a response. But the important thing is that we stand faithful to that hidden ground *alone*. We must trust the unseen.

So the contention of these pages is that there is within each of us a hidden life, a hidden ground of love which carries who we are. It is "hidden" in the sense that we have to trust that it is there. We cannot have direct sight of it. When we trust it then we know that it exists. All this is difficult because our eyes are fixed on the false and divisive realities of this world. These provide us with patterns of existence, protective coverings, controlling systems – more than we could ever need. We only adopt these patterns of value because we cannot see that the hidden ground of our being is love. Or perhaps we do and are unable to place our confidence in that apparently ephemeral and risky reality.

Kathleen Raine, one of our most distinguished contemporary poet/philosophers, describes the discovery of this apparently ephemeral reality as the true task of the poet. She calls it "The Hidden Journey of the Poet". This hidden journey finds some of its models in the journey of Dante into hell and Jung's journey to discover and own the shadow. The important point that Kathleen Raine makes is that the modern human condition is very much a *sleep*. We have forgotten our true selves, we have been lulled by a false consciousness, by modern waters of Lethe, into a sleep which we mistake for reality. The poet is the one who "remembers" and who by his speaking arouses his hearers, reawakens in them faded memories and sends them out on a journey into the true reality of the divine. Raine, like Iris Murdoch, places her trust in the power of works of genius to rouse us from sleep. ". . . such works," she says, "demand anamnesis, the wakening of recollection; and we might prefer to forget because sleep is easier and less demanding and sometimes less painful than wakefulness: which is nevertheless that to which we must grow."[10]

The task of the Church, and so the final purpose of all liturgy, prayer, preaching and the whole paraphernalia of the religious life, is no different. It is the task of "anamnesis" – a word, after all, beloved by liturgists – which is to provoke wakefulness to the truth about things. The task of the Church is to awaken people and society to their true condition as before God, to provide them with the environment within which "remembering" becomes possible and actual and then to sustain them on their journey back to the reality which they had forgotten.

This apparently simple, but in practice infinitely difficult, task means that Christian leaders of all kinds have to provide ways of provoking that insight in people, have to provide the means whereby they accept their nakedness, remember who they are, and so believe in God. So much of Christian life and worship does precisely the opposite, it provides something which is seen and comfortable rather than provoking people into stepping out into the unseen and taking the pain of the unseen upon themselves in the belief that this way is, in the end, health giving. We have to learn to trust that the hidden life of God is there, that he does live within us, and that this hidden presence is our final security and authority. We need nothing else. What appears from one side to be total spiritual nakedness, and therefore extremely daunting and very threatening, is, once accepted, the means of true fulfilment, where enjoyment of self, enjoyment of this world and of goodness, truth and beauty become both possible, natural and what we actually want. Most of us dispute this or cannot believe that it is possible, thinking that we are only our real selves when we cling on to what we have made of ourselves. God calls upon us not to cling to what we have made but to remember and to allow the hidden journey to commence. We have to wake up, to remember, to venture by trust into the unseen and the unknown, and to trust this journey is one which leads back to the truth which has been hidden from our eyes. We have to go back to the reality of love, God alone.

4

"I am invited to a party"

I still remember the first time I sailed to France. I was a schoolboy who suffered from a perilous attraction for the French language – my own not being interesting enough – and my school had arranged an exchange with a boy of similar age who lived in the south-west of France. I crossed the Channel on the overnight ferry from Southampton to Le Havre. I had decided to "rough it" – somehow this suited my self image at the time – and slept on the deck leaning against my bag. As we came into Le Havre the next morning I remember being dismayed by the dismal view of the town with its tall blocks of flats almost on the waterfront and the depressing quality of a channel port on a damp, overcast morning. It should be better than this, I thought. But things did get better. I had a day to explore Paris before the night train to Bordeaux, and found the Louvre and the Jardines des Tuileries and the boulevards and much else. Then out across France – Poitiers, Angoulême, Libourne, Bordeaux. An interminable wait and then out again into the sunshine of the Atlantic coast. I burst into the heat and light and the amused warmth of a French family. "Eat, eat", said the father as I nervously clutched a bowl of coffee and, for the occasion, a croissant.

Each of us has similar memories of setting out on

our first major expedition away from home. We all know when it happened first and can recall the tiny details of the first crossing, the first days at college, the first job. The experience of setting out seems to resonate within the human person with singular strength. "Setting out", although perilous, is deeply important. There is an enchanting and now classic account of this "setting out" by the travel writer, Patrick Leigh-Fermor, at the beginning of his book *A Time of Gifts* in which he describes how he walked across Europe as a young man. It is an account which seems to gather into itself the enthusiasm and pain of all the youthful expeditions that have ever been. Patrick Leigh-Fermor was a young man in London in the early thirties, and after a series of difficult and rather hesitant events decided, suddenly, to walk across Europe to Constantinople. "To change scenery; abandon London and England and set out across Europe like a tramp – or, as I characteristically phrased it to myself, like a pilgrim or a palmer, an errant scholar, a broken knight or the hero of *The Cloister and the Hearth*. All of a sudden this was not merely the obvious but the only thing to do. I would travel on foot, sleep in hayricks in summer, shelter in barns when it was raining or snowing and only consort with peasants and tramps . . . A new life! Freedom!"[1] The fact that the jaunt was so obviously romanticized, and that the author travelled with letters of introduction and so consorted as much with the fading and eccentric aristocracy of Europe as with tramps and peasants worries us not a jot. We recognize in his expedition something vital to the human spirit. It picks up within us something that we know. Setting out into the unknown in response to the call of the unknown is part of what it means to be and become a human being.

It should not surprise us to learn, therefore, that whereas we might understand such expeditions instinctively and write about them in a poetic vein, there are others who have understood this whole question of "setting out" not so much as a poetic whimsey but as an integral part of the intellectual tradition of western civilization. This way of looking at things opens up a complete anthropology around the idea that human beings are distinguished by their capacity to move forwards into the future. This capacity to entertain and respond to hope and freedom is what characterizes human beings and distinguishes them from other members of the animal kingdom. We are, as it were, *Homo Expectans* or *Homo Sperans*, always the ones who look towards the future. Human beings are those who are open to the future and who continually move towards it, creating new forms of society, new ways of being human, new ways of mirroring utopia at every step in the road. We are those beings who sense a certain incompleteness within themselves and who live, continually, by hope. Part of this way of seeing things, which incidentally, has been sadly out of fashion in English philosophical circles, dominated as they have been by the ghosts of logical positivism, understands that human beings continually need to create a new and just society in which to live. It is, then, a form of Marxist-humanism in which human beings are understood as necessarily moving towards a future in which oppression and injustice are no more. But this necessity is not derived from an analysis of history, as if history could create its own determining forces, but from something within the heart of humanity. It is an inborn and psychological necessity, a statement about how human beings are rather than an analysis of how history necessarily moves. That shift, from historical to psychological necessity, certainly brings this way of seeing things closer to home and makes it more accessible to the average English-speaking person with his or her inbuilt suspicions of continental and "Marxist" thinking. And in the end it makes a great deal of sense, given what is happening across the world, to understand ourselves in this way – as those who continually stand on the threshold, who are continually aware of our human and social incompleteness, continually looking for new horizons, new forms of social behaviour, new patterns which will accommodate the human spirit and enable the human race to live together in greater peace, justice and communal understanding.

Nor should Christians be very far behind in all this. For at the root of the Christian tradition stands Abraham, who set out from Ur of the Chaldees not knowing where he was going. Then follows Moses who led the people of Israel out into a new future, responding, like Abraham, to the call of God. Setting out into the unknown at the call of God is basic to the Judaeo-Christian understanding of how things are. This is what will come to the human person and this is what he must do if he wishes to remain human. All of our settings out, whether to France or across Europe or into a marriage or a new task, are but reflections, disguised images, of this primordial setting forth which lies buried in the heart of humankind. Only when we allow this setting forth to emerge within us and allow it to be a response to the call of God, will we discover our true identity.

For the urge to set forth is not our own, nor is it simply an empty movement, into nothing, a movement into absurdity. It is a setting forth in response to a summons, a call from outside, from the divine to the human person. It is a movement in response to an invitation. It is only at this point, and not before, that the Christian and the Marxist-humanist traditions will part company. The Marxist and the Christian will agree on the analysis so far, that human beings are essentially responsorial beings who, to be true to their own nature, continually need to move into the future creating ever more equitable ways of ordering their social existence. They should see this as a common platform, and share this common platform to engage in common endeavours for the betterment of social existence. The tragedy is that they do not even do that. They can and should act together. Where they will part company is on their understanding of the origin or source of the summons to justice.

This has been the point at which, during my time as a university chaplain, my left-wing conversation partners have felt obliged to draw stumps. Everything else is agreed, although some of them had never heard the Christian faith expounded in terms of a setting forth to establish the justice of the Kingdom before. Those who had, and who had been influenced by such a Kingdom theology in their youth, had sadly despaired of the capacity of the established Church to embody, realistically, such a way of seeing things in its life. This is really where the dialogue between the Church and the outsider should be taking place! For the Marxist-humanists, or at least those with whom I have discussed the matter, see the summons to human beings to move out into the future and to be engaged in the ever necessary task of recreating our social patterns so that we live in justice and peace, as simply being part of the phenomenon of human existence. Christians will understand the summons in personal terms, as springing from the origin and source of personality, God himself. The Marxist-humanist will shy away from this as being an unnecessary analysis, deriving from the projection of infantile human needs into the metaphysical sphere, a father figure in the sky that we don't really need. The Christian will reply that without the divine reference the motivation for human improvement will exhaust itself, the inspiration for new life will dry up and the path towards the achievement of this new life will be littered with unnecessary and bloody conflicts, unbridled violence and an unloving regard for those who stand in the path of progress. Unless there is a recognition that the invitation comes from God then the quest for utopia will be and remain just that.

Each of us, then, lives by call. The call comes to us both from outside of ourselves and, at the same time, from deep within ourselves, from deeper than our deepest self. It is the call of love. It is this call which summons us into existence, which both asks and enables us to stand on our own feet and to be ourselves, who we really are. It is this call which asks us to recognize that we are loved and wanted, needed even in the heart of what is at present unknown. The call comes to us from God, he who called creation into being at the beginning. Consequently, if the call remains the same now as it was then, it is not a call simply to exist. Existence is only the stage, the theatre for life, the raw material, the potter's clay. At the beginning God created by breathing life into what was formless, by letting his spirit blow across what was empty and void, by drawing order out of chaos. The call is the same now. It is a call into order from chaos, a call to purposefulness from inertia, it is a call to relatedness from isolation, it is a call to dignity from worthlessness, a call to participate in the making of things from a place where nothing was made. Human beings, if they believe in God, will allow that calling to exist in them, participate in it and allow themselves to be caught in its requirements.

Above all else this call is a call of love. It is not an impress, a moulding of basically recalcitrant material, a forcing of ways upon a humanity which is, at root, at enmity with the call which it hears. The only enmity which exists is that created by fear of the call itself. It does not demand what is not already there. It does not require anything that cannot be given. It does not require any response which it does not, before anything else happens, itself place within the heart of the one who is called. And so, in the truest sense, the call is really an invitation. Invitations are sent because of something which the sender recognizes in the life of the one he or she invites. They are a signal of possibilities. It is the same with God. He issues the invitation because he has already seen himself in us.

In the Garden of Eden God comes in the cool of the day and calls those whom he has already placed there: ". . . the Lord God called to the man and said to him,

'Where are you?'" That is the essential. God has already placed Adam and Eve in the garden. Indeed it was he who planted the garden and prepared it for them in the beginning. He knows who it is he has placed there. He has placed Adam and Eve there for companionship, both with each other and with himself. He has placed them there with the capacity not just to recognize who he is, but also to participate in his activity. He has given to Adam the capacity to participate in the very act of calling itself. Adam is made so that he can be part of what it is that God does. Having called the universe, and then the garden and then Adam into existence, God gives that same task over to him. "So God formed out of the ground all the wild animals and all the birds of heaven. He brought them to the man to see what he would call them, and whatever the man called each living creature, that was its name."[2]

The nature of God is to create in such a way that what he has created then itself bears the creative role. He does not just make, he makes things that make. He has not created in order to dominate and subdue, but so that what is made may share in the very process of creation itself. God brings the creatures that he has made to mankind and accepts the names that they are given; and in the understanding of the Old Testament authors the name is not just a word it is also the identity. So the call which God utters when he comes into the garden in the cool of the evening cannot, if we give it thought, be a call which contains any kind of threat. It is not a source of alienation. The call is itself a promise, an intimation of possibilities. It contains the possibility of knowing that human beings have been made in love and are themselves able to share in the creative possibilities of love. This is the call, to be what we have already been made.

In the Gospels Jesus issues to the disciples precisely the same invitation that God issued to Adam at the beginning. It is an invitation to come and follow, but also an invitation to participate in the work which he had to do. Having been called the disciples are then sent out to do that which Jesus himself continues to do. There is a distinct point in Luke's Gospel, for instance, where Jesus calls the disciples together and gives them the same authority which Luke, up to that point, has described Jesus himself as possessing. The whole burden of Jesus' teaching at the end of St John's Gospel is that the disciples have to bear the divine life themselves once Jesus has physically left them. The disciples themselves do not see this easily, and some of Jesus' sharpest rebukes are reserved for their lack of faith in what he has called them to be. They are unable to see what it is they really are except by answering the invitation.

When it is answered the disciples discover that the call of Jesus is a call which was already present, as it were, within them and is awakened, or rather their memory of it is awakened, by his presence. The Gospels portray the disciples as answering the call of Jesus with great promptness, leaving their nets "at once". The invitation strikes a chord in their hearts which they recognize and own immediately. I used to be taught in Sunday School that this was because Jesus had already visited the disciples and talked with them, so that when he came by they were responding to a pre-arranged signal! I know now that their response is portrayed in this way because the Evangelists themselves knew how the call of Christ resonated deep within their own experience. It was not an intellectual choice and could not be portrayed in rational terms. In St John's Gospel the process of recognition is described at greater length towards the end of chapter one. In this passage first the two disciples of John, then Peter and then Philip and Nathanael are all called. All of them recognize in Jesus what they have already been looking for. They say, "We have found the Messiah". The call of Nathanael is even more pregnant with meaning. The fact that Nathanael was seen by Jesus "under the fig tree" emphasizes both that Jesus has seen him before but also that he has been "seen" before by God, and that what is happening is part of what was destined to happen to Nathanael from the beginning. It also emphasizes that God has seen us and loved us before, that he calls that which is his own. And in case we missed it all this is made quite explicit in the opening words of the Gospel, where it says, "He was in the world; but the world, though it owed its being to him, did not recognize him." In other words the call of Jesus is a call to recognize that your being is derived from God, from the one who issues the call. Those who respond are responding to the call of their innermost nature, and by responding signal their discovery that this innermost nature itself derives from God.

I have emphasized that the invitation of God is a promise and that response to it involves a recognition of our true nature and issues in a flowering of who we were created to be because I know that so many understand it as a threat. For them it is a demand. It is a call which requires total submission. And there is an increasing contemporary interest in submission. Fundamentalism requires submission. Those who accept submission are only too prone to pass this submission on to others, and the links between submission in religion and the adoption of an oppressive state regime in the history as well as in the contemporary practice of Christianity are all too plain. But Christianity has never been a religion of submission. It is a religion of the invitation of love. In one sense the invitation of God is a continual song within us, a song which invites us to respond not by submission, as if the song were elsewhere and we had to listen and learn, but by participation, because the song is within us. Those who call for submission do so because for them the call of God only comes from without, as if the human person were incapable of bearing something of the life of God already. The scriptural witness and the experience of the Church is that the invitation is addressed to those whom God already knows, those in whom his life already exists and has existed from the beginning. This is the source of the response but also the cause of the invitation. Above all else it is an invitation to recognize what God has been doing within you from the very beginning.

But there is still more. In Merton's dream he is invited to a party. It is a party with fine people, well dressed in an attractive setting, and, he says, "I am invited to the party with them . . ."

The consciousness of most people in the West is that they are separate. The prevailing experience seems to be that human beings are like a clutch of children's balloons, all bumping against one another. Each of us has our own separate shape, colour and size. This is our immediate consciousness and it is one we are determined to maintain. The prevailing ideology of our Western democracies is individualistic. Governments are determined to maintain the centrality of individual choice, both as a political and as a philosophical option. But there is another consciousness, one of a quite different kind, which breaks through from time to time. Try asking a young couple with their first child, for example, where each of their personalities begins and ends. The question will appear absurd. Try asking lovers about their distinct selves and they will not understand. Try asking a long-married couple about their individual personalities and they will reply that their present personalities are as much the product of their unity as anything else. For them they are each who they are as a result of their unity. Their individual selves and, consequently, their individual choices, are derivative. Participation comes first. Nor is this experience limited to those who are married or in love. John Taylor, who later became Bishop of Winchester, spent a long period of his early life in Uganda and speaks very movingly of the way in which the Africans he lived with had a deep sense of belonging together. Individual personality was merged into a sense of corporate consciousness. He writes, for example, of a fishing trip he made on Lake Victoria and of the experience of working with the fishermen to the point where the edges of individual consciousness began to melt away.

It is this sense of being first of all a corporate being that we have betrayed to the Western individualized

consciousness. In our present world we perceive ourselves as individuals, owning, making, possessing,
doing, choosing. We think, quite naturally, that it is
individuals who can make unity. Unity derives from
individuals who decide to work together for that end.
This is an unquestioned assumption which does not
apply in the technologically unsophisticated parts of
the world and which did not always apply in the West.
It is, effectively, an invention of the European mind
since Descartes. But the truth is otherwise. Unity is
the prior gift. The individual is derivative from that
prior ground. It is within that unity that the individual
operates. He does not own it and so cannot make it or
not make it as the mood takes him. The realization
that this is true is actually a liberation and brings us
into touch with the roots of our being and with God.
The burdens of individualistic achievement then drop
away and we can actually become who we are as
persons much more easily and freely than before. An
acceptance of unity as the prior gift allows the individual to flourish. The disasters come when this individual
flourishing begins to take precedence over the corporate life of which it is simply the fruit. We have
forgotten how to stop that happening. In his extraordinary account of his work amongst the Masai
people of East Africa, Father Vincent Donovan shows
how that tribe saw the dangers and acted to preserve
unity in the face of growing individualism. He
recounts how he was preparing a group for baptism.
Towards the end of their preparation he said that he
thought some could not be baptized. This was either
because they had not attended all of the classes or
because he felt that they had not grasped the Christian

message sufficiently well. This met with great protest. The old man of the group stepped forward. "Yes", he said, "there are stupid ones in the community, but they have been helped by those who are intelligent. Yes, there are ones with little faith in this village, but they have been helped by those with much faith." And so the whole group was baptized because of their communal faith. It was, as Father Donovan admitted, an example of the triumph of African corporate awareness over Western individual choice.[3]

All of this reflects the earlier Christian view that human beings belong to each other first and are individuals second. "We are members one of another." In the fourth century St Ambrose speaks against private property, calling it a form of theft. The call of God is a call to recognize that human beings derive their capacity to exist from an acceptance of their incompleteness as individuals. Human identity derives from our acceptance of our corporate participation in the human race and so in the love of God. We are members of this family first, first we are sharers, first we are participators. We are individuals only because we allow that to be the case.

It is our inability to accept this which makes the Christian doctrine of the Trinity such a difficult one. For most people belief in God as Trinity is an intellectual conundrum. We have to reconcile threeness and oneness. Various simple images, like clover leaves or triangles are suggested in order to help us understand the conundrum. But the problem arises only because of the way the matter is put. We are asked to give intellectual assent to a belief. We should, but usually are not, be asked to allow ourselves to live within God and to allow his divinity to live within us. The Christian belief in the Trinity is, in reality, an affirmation of the nature of the life of the baptized – that he or she as an individual participates in the unitive life of God. Assent to the doctrine of the Trinity is not an intellectual matter at all, it is, rather, an affirmation about our life. It is a consent, rather than an assent, which we give to the unity and divinity within us; our consent to participation in the communal and participatory nature of the divine life.

Once this is allowed, that the source of human identity lies within the apparent abandonment of identity to the life of God within, then a number of things follow. In the first place we will begin to see a way of resolving our intellectual difficulties over the faith. We will move from the need to test and criticize to the need to live the doctrines we profess. Such a movement can only be a sign of maturity. So much Western Christianity is still caught in the immaturity of asking questions rather than the maturity of allowing and encouraging consent to occur within the human psyche. Secondly we will come to a deep personal sense of inner acceptance and thankfulness. This thankfulness for all that is will then, in its turn, draw us into the central action of humanity, the action of adoration.

There is within each of us both a call and a consent. We have to hear the call and allow the consent in order to become fully human. The call is from God. The consent has been within us from the beginning. It is a primordial "yes", and we have to allow that "yes" to answer.

"To assume that my superficial ego – this cramp of

the imagination – is my real self is to begin by dishonouring myself and reality."

"We must go back to the beginning."

"If we take a more living and more Christian perspective we find in ourselves a simple affirmation which is not of ourselves. It simply *is*. In our being there is a primordial *yes* that is not our own . . ."

"Practical conclusion: one must learn to live and act not merely on the basis of ideological principles which seem to suit one's own sense of identity and which enable one to make plausible adjustments between 'yes' and 'no'. One must live as a Christian, act as a Christian, with a life and an activity which spring from the unconditional 'yes' of Christ to the Father's will, incarnated in our own unconditional 'yes' to the reality, truth, and love which are made fully accessible to us in the Person and in the Cross of Christ." [4]

"... and suddenly they are all gone"

One of the interesting and exciting things about being a university chaplain was the onset of the new academic year. What would it bring? What sort of students would come? What would they be like this time? It was hard work too, for after saying farewell in July to a large proportion of my congregation – whom I had got to know well over the last three years – it was now time to make friends with a new batch. All of my tact and understanding would be needed. Some of the new ones would find relationships with the chaplain easy, and would come looking, especially if they were used to a strong church life at home and had been servers or choir members. Others would find it difficult or impossible and shy away directly. Some would pour out their problems, both real and assumed, without any prompting; others would wait.

Mingled with their reaction to the presence of a chaplain was their reaction – more important – to life at university. The first term is always exciting. I can only remember one student in twelve years who reacted badly to the first term – and her problems were nothing to do with universities. But the second and third terms are different, more costly, difficult to handle. By this time they have all become aware of how little money they have and just how far it has to go. Their friendship groups are beginning to form in a more realistic way. Who they really want to know is either there or in another group. Choices about who to go about with become very alarming. Work begins to be more of a chore and then the question of where to live in the second year becomes a major problem. It is at some point in this part of the academic year too that the student has to come to grips with the question of his or her relationship with home. A small number never actually face this problem and remain permanently locked into an adolescent relationship with their mother or father. Some may reconcile themselves to the break with home but reconstitute their adolescent relationship with the chaplain or a tutor. Others, usually the vast majority, move with a variety of growing pains into adult autonomy.

But at some point during this period there will come a moment for every student when they realize that they are actually on their own. Home is no longer able to provide them with the same degree of protection and security. Their college or university will only be able to replace this security in a very limited sense, and then not for very long. They have friends, but soon realize that they cannot make their choices for them. They have to find their own way. It is at this point that a very important thing happens. The student comes face to face with his or her own loneliness. They are faced with solitude. This is the most important point, for what they do now, how they react to this experience – for it will be repeated, especially if they shrink from it now – will determine how they are and especially how they are before God for a very long time to come. A great deal of Christian chaplaincy work makes a massive mistake at this point by trying to provide the means whereby the student can be sheltered or protected from this awesome moment. Peer groups are provided. Parties are arranged. Chaplains work themselves into the ground being a friend to everyone, doing immensely good work, but often simply reinforcing the student's flight from his loneliness. A number of things can happen at this juncture. The student may interpret this moment negatively, seeing it as a moment of despair, a glimpse of *le néant*. He or she may conclude from this that there is no God, that we are each left alone and unsupported by any outside being or agency. On the whole, whether articulated or not, this is the more common conclusion. It appears to produce two types of behaviour pattern, or rather a single pattern with two sides to it. This is a pattern which exhibits despair and depression accompanied by antipathetic social behaviour on the one hand, and frenzied involvement in human relationships, sometimes of a very tangled nature, on the other. Manic swings occur from hyper-activity to solipsistic and anti-social isolationism. But for all, whatever their point on the pendulum, "being kind" is extremely important, probably because there is very little else; but this kindness often breaks down, especially in the face of urgent personal needs, because there is no real reason to be kind except kindness itself. Kindness is adopted as a philosophy because there is no other. But it is a kindness which relies entirely on the human psyche for its generation and sustenance. There is no transcendent source of human kindness outside the human self. Is this perhaps the reason for the extreme violence with which many young people join the anti-vivisectionist movement? It is an expression of kindness, but made violent because of the metaphysical despair which provokes and accompanies it. As far as students are concerned, however, the vast majority react to their sense of cosmic loneliness by a resolve to "get on". Achievement, not in the academic sphere, for that is infinitely boring, but in the world of their chosen career, is the be-all and end-all. This will relieve them of their malaise.

Another reaction, less common, to the sense of being alone is the religious equivalent to what I have already described. The student becomes religious. He or she begins to attend Bible study groups, prayer meetings and Christian Union meetings without ceasing. All of this type of student's friends are Christian. Indeed, having friends who are not Christian has become a theological problem which is discussed at great length in these meetings. There is no meeting with the secular world. It is declared to be empty, or "fallen", a declaration which is more likely to be a projection of the student's own sense of emptiness and loneliness than to have anything to do with the world itself. The interesting thing about this rejection of the world is that it seldom, if ever, takes the form of a rejection of the world's *material* values. Generally speaking the young evangelical Christian of today believes in his or her right to a good salary, and will reject quite fiercely the arguments of the Gospels about the need for simplicity and poverty in our lives. What *is* rejected is all personal and sexual behaviour which is found to be threatening and which is claimed to be deviant. There is for these young Christians a strong corporate behaviour pattern based, ostensibly, on commitment to Jesus Christ, but which contains a number of social attitudes which are very far from the attitudes which Christ himself exhibited towards those who did not fit in to the society of his time. Such behaviour patterns are a religious version of the secular pattern we outlined above. It contains a deep and frenzied striving for acceptance and belonging which is couched in religious terminology. It also contains a great deal of anguish about the state of the soul, which again is often little more than depression in the face of loneliness transmuted into religious language. Certainly happiness and self-acceptance are seldom hallmarks of this group.

Both of these groups, the secular and the religious, are reacting in basically similar ways to a common factor. This common factor is the discovery of solitude within the human psyche. The secular reaction is at least honest – dismay and disarray. The apparently religious reaction is culpable on a number of points. It encourages the belief that religion exists to save one from this experience. Religion, it is thought, saves one from solitude. It enables you to "belong" – that blessed condition. That acceptance of the experience of solitude might be religiously valuable is a notion that cannot be entertained. That solitude might not be the same thing as isolation, and that solitude might be an intrinsic strand in the Judaeo-Christian tradition and, furthermore, that the apparent absence of God might be an important *religious* notion in both Christian and Jewish thought has not yet dawned on their consciousness. We ought, perhaps, to look more closely at the formation we provide for the young of the Church, for my experience is that there is very little awareness among them of the importance of self acceptance nor very much acceptance of the notion of the absence of God. This latter point can be illustrated by a conversation I had with a devout Christian student about the absence of God. I was pointing out that whereas most contemporary talk about God emphasizes his presence to the believer and the importance of religious experience, this needs to be balanced against a longstanding tradition of experience of the absence of God. I explained the Via Negativa and described the poetry of St John of the Cross, and referred to the biblical experience of God being "hidden" – "Verily thou art a God that hidest thyself". I still remember clearly the student's puzzled and uncomprehending reaction. This was certainly not the Christianity she wanted – which probably says it all.

I have described all this at some length because I believe that the dilemma of our students and their failure to understand that the "wilderness point" in their experience is God given, only pinpoints the dilemma of all of us. Students, as so often in the history of Europe, symbolize the problems we all face and reflect back to us, as in a mirror, where we are all going. For them, as for us, true dignity as religious human beings does not lie in fleeing before the discovery of our loneliness into social hedonism or various types of panic. Nor does it consist in the religious equivalent – furious searching for true experience, as if religion were just another possession to be acquired, and God were there waiting to be touched. True religious and human dignity lies rather in recognizing that it is within this moment, when suddenly "they are all gone", that the greatest religious opportunity arises.

For it is at this point that God, who is always unseen, is closest. It is at this point that we have to remain. It is this point that we even have to plunge into in order to discover that this *néant*, this apparent nothingness, holds within it the secret of the heart of God. It appears to be darkness and silence. In fact it is the silence of love. The existentialist interprets this silence as "nothing". The secularist flees from it as being the edge of the map. The Christian believes that it contains God. Francis Thompson's poem, "The Hound of Heaven", illustrates the dilemma very well. Most of the time, he says, we flee, but cannot easily escape what appears to be a deeply negative force. The answer lies in turning to accept. Then we will say, in wonder, "Is my gloom but the shade of thy hand, outstretched caressingly."

This point, which all of us reach eventually, when we say, "they have all gone away", is not a negative point. It is the point at which we are given the opportunity to face God and can return knowing that we need nothing else. It is at this point that our maturity as persons begins. It is from this point that we can turn and face our experiences and our relationships with complete inner confidence, realizing that we are not dependent upon them for our identity. That is given us by God. Nor is God seen at this point, for it remains true even at this moment of apparent solitude that our knowledge of God is not direct or immediate. Our knowledge of God is always mediated to us. It is simply that the means of mediation is solitude. Nor is this a vindication of isolationism or solipsism or anything similar. Just the contrary, for it is here that we recognize our dependence upon and our participation in everything else. Everything is dependent and we are happily dependent within that pattern of things. Our experience of isolation will be seen to derive from a rejection of that beautiful and humbling truth. We feel isolated because we are not confident enough to accept that when apparent isolation comes upon us it is simply a door through which we have to step. When we step through it we find ourselves within the fellowship of all things. It is at this point that we discover that whereas we had thought that we were totally alone, if we turn and accept that loneliness as gift, then we will come to know that we were not alone at all but part of the universe. In this way loneliness will be turned into solitude.[1] It is as if we have to go into the wilderness in order to discover that no wilderness, except that of our own making, exists. The wilderness is created by our own fear of it all. But this is an insight derived from looking back, from hindsight. The important thing to realize is that if we, on arrival at the wilderness point, decide to hang on to it, decide that it is so real that all of our actions will be governed by its impact, then the consequence will be that we shall enter into one or other of those patterns of existence which my students mirrored for me so exactly. What we have to do is grasp the isolation, grasp the experience which threatens to destroy by its intense loneliness, and see it as gift, the gift of God to us. Here at this point God is speaking. "Behold I will lure her into the wilderness and speak gently to her".[2] But unfortunately we are usually too busy experiencing the wilderness as pain to see the gift that it contains.

It is at this wilderness point that we might, if we are patient in suffering, come to see that our sense of separation is not real, but alien. It derives either from the social conditions under which we live or from our own fears and fantasies. Most likely it is a combination of both. We experience separation, but it is an experience produced for us by the conditions of life. It is, in fact, a form of illusion. The truth is that the separation is unreal, experienced, but not what is. So from our experience of finding God in the wilderness we can draw conclusions about the nature of existence. The religious tradition in which Christians stand should help them to understand all this. That tradition speaks very clearly of the influence of the "powers, dominions and authorities" of this world and of the way in which human beings can be subject to them. This subjection is caused by the illusions which we have about ourselves and is then reinforced by our refusal to abandon them, even when exposed as such. And so when Christianity speaks of a flight from the world or a separation from the world in order to be with God, what is really meant is that the Christian should free himself or herself from the illusion of what this world can do and be. What actually separates us from the reality of God – and we should be in no doubt that the experience is extremely sharp and at times very bitter – is not so much the evil world in which we live or even the sinfulness of our behaviour. The world is not evil as such and our sinfulness is the result of our lack of faith and trust. No, what brings about the separation is a set of illusions about ourselves and about our place in the world. Those illusions in their turn then bring about evil and sinful behaviour. We are victims of illusions about ourselves, about the world and our place in it, about the status of our rational understanding of this world and what that rational understanding can do and so on. We are in fact the victims of pride, the biggest illusion of them all. It is from this illusion that we must be liberated and not the world itself. Once we are free from it we shall be able to see who we really are and how we can, gladly, be part of things as they are.

Thomas Merton talks about all this in an essay he wrote called, *Is the World a Problem?* He says, "for anyone who has seriously entered into the medieval Christian, or Hindu, or the Buddhist conceptions of *contemptus mundi, Mara* or '*the emptiness of the world*', it will be evident that this means not the rejecting of a reality but the unmasking of an illusion. The world as pure object is something that is not there. It is not a reality outside us for which we exist . . . if anything, the world exists for us, and we exist for ourselves." He continues a few sentences later to talk about "the reality" of the world which interpenetrates us. "This reality, though 'external' and 'objective', is not something entirely independent of us, which dominates us inexorably from without through the medium of certain fixed laws which science alone can discover and use. It is an extension and projection of ourselves and of our lives, and if we attend to it respectfully, while attending also to our own freedom and our own integrity, we can learn to obey its ways and to co-ordinate our lives with its mysterious movements. The way to find the real 'world' is not merely to measure and observe what is outside us, but to discover our own inner ground . . . when I find the world in my own ground it is impossible for me to be alienated by it."[3]

This is an important and neglected passage in Merton's writings. Important not just for the light which it sheds on the estimate we have of the "objectivity" of the scientific method and of the false distinctions we make between our interior and exterior lives, but also for the way in which it gently levers us away from thinking of ourselves as beings which are distinct from another reality, over which we hover like some spy satellite in the metaphysical sky, watching whatever is going on below. At the wilderness point we have the opportunity to realize that we are in God and he in us. If at this point we continue to fight for our own independence then we shall never enter into the life of God. We might continue to believe in him as an objective reality, but we shall be unable to surrender ourselves to the fact that he is, and so our belief, however correctly argued, will remain sterile and refuse to communicate itself to others. Merton says the same thing when he says we are self-alienating. We allow ourselves to be governed and controlled by a set of illusions which we then say are "reality". We give a totally unreal identity to a particular set of imperatives and then say that we have to live by them. We create our own alienation and then lie down under it, complaining bitterly. For Merton salvation means discovering that you have done this and then allowing that discovery to set you free from the power that these imperatives exert. These imperatives are so often given the status of a value system, "our" value system, and observed as the values we need to live by, when in actual fact our true values, the ones we have had within us from the beginning, are hidden and forgotten, put aside, repressed. What we need to do is to rediscover a sense of confidence in what we have been given, what Merton calls our own "inner ground". We have to allow ourselves to be carried on a hidden journey. The wilderness point is the point at which we come face to face with the hidden nature of this journey and either acknowledge that we live by powers unknown, and so are led into fruitfulness, happiness and a relationship with the creation and the creator, or continue to fight for control and end up terrified, desperately seeking more and more power in order to control the beasts which we have projected into a reality of our own making. The preoccupation of the Western individual and the Western nations with the notions of power and control, together with all the suffering and destruction that stems from that preoccupation, is one direct result of our corporate refusal to face the invisibility of God at the point of wilderness. Political conflict does therefore need spiritual discernment if it is to be properly and completely understood and expunged. Political answers must be sought, but never in isolation from spiritual awareness.

Let me illustrate all this with a story of two people who found themselves alone. In the story of Adam and Eve in the book of Genesis, Eve is tempted by the serpent and then Adam eats. "Then the eyes of both of them were opened, and they knew that they were naked; and they sewed fig leaves together and made themselves aprons." At this point God comes into the garden and calls them, but they hide away. Adam says, "I heard the sound of thee in the garden and I was afraid, because I was naked; and I hid myself". And then God asks the most important question of all, one which everybody who comes to the wilderness point has to ask. It is a deeply human and searching question, and the answer we give it will determine the whole shape of our lives. For none of us is apparently able to abide the discovery of our own nakedness as people. We quickly become frightened and grasp at the nearest and most convenient fig leaf with which to cover ourselves. We invent schemes, value systems, patterns of living because we cannot stand before the fire of God alone. And when the fire of God burns away what we have invented and asks, "Do you love me more than these?", we are angry and rebel and ask to return to the land whence we came. In particular the religious person reinforces his pattern of living with a set of religious practices which then in turn become inviolable, even when the way of life which they accompanied and supported has disappeared. We don't seem to be able to sit lightly to our traditions, recognizing that they are there to enable men and women to find God but that he is greater than any of them. We cannot be naked, and when God asks us why we cannot be naked we tend to become defensive and even imply that God should support what we are doing because we are doing it for his sake! But the question is relentless – "Who told you that you were naked?" God pushes us, gently but very firmly, to ask ourselves what force it is, what power it is that has usurped his dominion and authority within our lives and persuaded us that we need some protective covering. Are we not perfectly acceptable in our original nakedness? In the end it is our inability to cope with the threat of our own nakedness which is the root of tragedy and disaster in human experience. It is certainly the inability to face that threat which is the root of fascism. It is this inability which drives us out of the Garden of Eden into a world of our own making. We seem to prefer the certainties of our own power conflicts to the uncertainties of trust and faith. We need to relearn that we do not need any covering. Making fig leaves is the beginning of alienation from the inner ground of our being, which is love.

All this is of immense importance for the future of humanity. So much of what we are now is at risk. We could lose ourselves. This is sensed by the most ordinary people. One of my staff remarked the other day, "It's as if Britain needs to have somebody come along and shake it by the scruff of its neck. We all need a good shaking." I think she felt that we had lost or risked losing our way, that we had lost sight of those values, values such as goodness, honesty, truth and the like, by which ordinary people live and find happiness. These have all been sold to alien values such as greed and success, interlopers into the human soul. For the important thing to realize is that the values by which human beings find happiness are not, in the long run, imposed or acquired, as if there were a range of values on offer and the human soul could choose and was empty until filled up with the right ones.

The values or identities we need are not contrived or imposed. They derive from within, from the ground of our being, which is love. They are already there and need to be allowed to emerge from behind the illusions adopted out of fear or greed. These values operate when human beings accept that the ground of their being is the mystery of love, and when they trust that those with whom they are engaged, their neighbours and friends, also have love as the ground of their being. This trust will then, all being well, call out love in our neighbours and friends in response to our expressed love. It may not, but the important thing is that we stand faithful to that inner ground of love alone. This is really only another way of saying that we must believe in God and not in idols. It is a mistake to assume that we Western people are now educated and free from idolatry – the contrary seems to be the case. We have too many idols. The expression of formal belief in God is only an intellectual statement of the interior acceptance of the ground of our being as all-sufficient. It needs belief in God to be that trusting! We do not need anything else. We have to accept our own nakedness, our original condition, as being perfectly sufficient. Once we begin to think that this needs some sort of covering, that it is not enough, or cannot be trusted, then we have lost the battle for the self and are on our way out of the garden. When that abandonment occurs, when we cover our nakedness, when we turn away from the incandescent flame within as being too bright, when we prefer lesser jewels, then the hidden journey is totally forgotten and a visible, indeed highly visible, journey has taken its place.

The values and identities we adopt must, therefore, spring from who we really are, and not from a hurriedly acquired and rather fashionable set of fig leaves. This requires an acceptance of our original nakedness and so appears at first sight to be extremely daunting and very threatening. Remaining at the wilderness point does not look, on the face of it, very comfortable. But actually, once accepted, this is the means of fulfilment, the point at which enjoyment of the self, enjoyment of this world and the acceptance of goodness, truth and beauty become both possible, natural and what we discover we want. This is a form of mysticism, a mysticism for city dwellers, for suburbanites, for those who feel surrounded by so much. It is certainly a negative way, a refusal of all the palliatives of modern life, a refusal of all easy answers, of ecclesiastically laundered fig leaves, until only God is reached. In the end no mysticism is really barren. The mysterious ground of our being is love, not emptiness. This is the final distinction – and there are many similarities – between Christianity and existentialism. Both understand that *le néant* is central to human experience, but whereas for one it is seen as a true emptiness, for the other to step into it is to step into life. Edward Schillebeeckx, the contemporary theologian, makes this clear when he says, "Mysticism in no way means 'God and only God'. St Francis's hymn to the sun makes that clear when St Francis says, 'Be praised, my Lord, with all your creatures!' The mystic first of all wants to let everything go, everything including himself or herself, but in the grace of God he get everything back a hundredfold, himself or herself included. Genuine mysticism is never a flight from the world."[4]

The question, "Who told you that you were naked?" is a subversive one. It takes us to the root of things and asks us to accept the authority of the ground of our being as final.

6

"I have five dollars"

The son of some friends of ours recently spent a summer in the United States. He worked, as many young people do, with *Camp America*, looking after smaller children in vacation camps. During his stay he travelled widely, seeing America by Greyhound bus. However much he saw he still found himself being drawn back not to a spectacle or a man-made wonder, but to a way of life. This was the way of life led by the Amish communities of Pennsylvania and Ohio. These communities were invited to settle in Pennsylvania by William Penn's sons in 1727. They share an anabaptist heritage with the Mennonites and have preserved their ethnic and religious identities over against the way of the world. They live in simplicity and, as far as possible, in self-sufficiency. "Our Way", as the Amish call it, is a radical return to a biblically based life style. This leads them to a rejection of electricity, the maintenance of horse-drawn farming methods and transport, their own schools, the minimal use of the petrol engine, plain dress – without zippers or buttons, both regarded as "fancy" – and the rejection of wardrobes or curtains in the home. These "plain folk" order both their lives and their land with simplicity of means – but there is a beauty in their plainness which is reflected in their gardens and in their highly prized hand-sewn quilts. Plainness does not mean ugliness. The basis of Amish society can be seen from the decision of the Supreme Court, made in 1972, to exempt the Amish from the necessity of attending state-maintained High School. Chief Justice Warren Burger then wrote, "Amish objection to formal education beyond the eighth grade is firmly grounded in central religious beliefs ... the High School tends to emphasize intellectual and scientific accomplishments, self-distinction, competitiveness, worldly success and social life with other students. Amish society emphasizes informal learning-through-doing; a life of goodness, rather than a life of intellect; wisdom rather than technical knowledge; community welfare rather than competition; and separation, rather than integration with contemporary world society."

Our friends' son, Jonathan, was fascinated by this society and on his return from America announced his desire to go back to work for a while with the Amish communities. What had impressed him, he said, was their refusal to accept the all-prevailing materialism of American society. In conversation he reminded us of the film "Witness", which portrays a young boy who has witnessed a murder and who takes refuge among the Amish, and the impact his film had upon young people of his generation.

As we were reflecting on his recognition that the Amish communities pointed to something desperately lacking in Western society, my wife and I watched a television programme on the life and work of Mother Teresa of Calcutta. We saw her sisters, the Missionaries of Charity, setting up home in one of the great cities of America. A church there had provided them with a house, fully furnished and complete with carpets and central heating. The carpets were rolled up and thrown out of the windows. We then watched the incomprehending expression on the face of the heating engineer who, after he had extolled the virtues of his system, was gently told by a sari-clad American sister, 'I don't think we'll need that'. Poverty of life style, as Mother Teresa explained later in the film, enabled her sisters to be truly free for the poor. We saw a young English woman, who had been a well-paid literary agent in London, making her vows and dedicating herself to a lifetime of ministering to the poorest of the poor. Was it a waste or was it a recognition by her of an inadequacy in Western society, an emptiness in the midst of success which could only be fulfilled by a life of self-abandonment?

The curious thing about each of these incidents was the reaction they provoked. Jonathan's experiences were the subject of much dinner table talk. Mother Teresa and her Missionaries of Charity provoke both admiration and sharp disagreement, as I discovered when I talked about the programme with some Catholic friends whom I thought would be sympathetic. But neither the Amish nor Mother Teresa were ignored. It is as if their behaviour acts as a catalyst for the grave dilemmas we face, provoking us to find better answers, clearer responses, rather than complacent acceptance of our present condition. Each of these incidents brings something into focus. We face a dilemma, although we may not recognize it, because of our materialism. We have assumed that the acquisition of possessions, whether physical, intellectual or religious, will provide us with the good life. We are deeply puzzled when this is questioned and resist the call to abandon or share what we own. This resistance, every time it is made, then reinforces our inability to allow the life of the spirit to take priority in our way of living. We find ourselves looking at the Amish way of life in wonder and fear. Our fear may lead us to criticism, finding their ways negative or repressive, but we also have the niggling recognition that there is a deeper capacity for contentment in the way that they follow. We look in wonder at Mother Teresa, but we are deeply unable, unwilling even, to allow that type of spirituality to invade our existence even in the smallest degree. It is somehow acceptable for her to live like that, but absurd for us. We cannot easily incorporate the values which motivate her behaviour into our own lives. And in some of the conversations which we had after listening to Jonathan or watching Mother Teresa, there was even a clear recognition that we were trapped into being like we are, a recognition that we have allowed the trap to operate and even, to some extent, are happy with it because it is fur lined. This is a clear but honest recognition of defeat at the hands of the powers of the world.

But then, in reflecting on all this, I came to the conclusion that, in a curious kind of way, materialism was not the real problem. Religious people tend to inveigh, often quite heavily, against "materialism" and place it in simple opposition to "a spiritual way of life". This, I began to feel, is to oversimplify. Materialism is perceived as the problem, but it is actually the presenting symptom of a more deep-seated disease. The root problem lies further back than the simple question of acquiring material goods. We have, I think, lost our capacity for discernment over the possession and use of things, whether these things are money or clothes or nuclear weapons or the precious possessions of mind and heart. This lost capacity has been occasioned by two shifts of attitude which most people have taken on board. The first is that we now assume, quite clearly, that possession is a natural and inalienable right. The second is the assumption that we have, once in possession of a thing, the natural and morally justified right to use that thing. Both of these shifts have occurred almost without comment and both represent a very considerable shift away from the earlier Christian tradition. When they occurred is impossible to define accurately, but it is clear that they are associated with the rise of individualism and the decline of a deep sense not just of corporate belonging but of corporate responsibility in society. The rise of individualism is itself a product of the Enlightenment, a movement which had its roots in the disintegration which occurred in Europe in the sixteenth century. How these shifts occurred is important but here we are concerned with their results. There is, for example, a debate over the possession and use of nuclear weapons by the technologically advanced nations of the world. This debate, however important in itself, is only one of so many debates which we conduct about possession and use in general. We appear to have moved, slowly but surely, into an assumption that individual possession is an inalienable right. To question this right to possession and use by the individual has become an abuse of the freedom of the individual by the state. Those who attempt to exercise controls over the individual's assumed right to possession and use risk being branded as Communists. We are deeply protective of our own right to possess and extremely glad, as well as not a little relieved, when we see evidence in communist countries that they too desire individual possessions. This is what human beings were made for. Our understanding of human nature has moved to accept the hidden assumption that human beings naturally need to possess things and to thwart this natural right is to go against nature. Meanwhile the religious life, which traditionally has a great deal to say about possessions, has come to be regarded as something which concerns itself with the personal and private realm of religious experience. In contemporary society religion is a matter of private experience or personal opinion. In the popular, secular imagination it has the same status as any other hobby. It is all right if you happen to need it. Religion is for the elderly or the sick or the weak-minded. Those who have grown up do not need it. In any case, even when acquired, it is clearly unable to say very much about how we own things or what we should do with what we own.

In contemporary society religion is to do with experience, or, to put it more clearly, with experiences – experiences of the divine, or of the demonic, or of the friendship of Jesus, or of the overwhelming power of the master guru. This evacuation of the moral or religious significance of possession and ownership has the terrible consequence that possession of any kind has become a totally uncontrolled phenomenon. We think we need possessions in order to be human, and in so thinking allow ourselves to be possessed by whatever it is that we desire. Possession is uncontrolled in terms of what we think we can own – and for evidence of that we have only to listen to the news reports of what has happened to consumer spending as a phenomenon in contemporary society. It is also uncontrolled in personal and psychological terms. "Possession" as a phenomenon in the Western mentality is not subject to any form of control. Our video shops – an important indicator of our inner and largely hidden condition – are full of films about "possession" of one kind or another, whether possession by alien forces from another planet, or possession by evil forces from the unknown, or possession by some psychological disorder. This preoccupation by possession exercises a curious fascination, compounded by terror, which in the end can only be a sign of the emptiness of our inner life. In fact, by abandoning our capacity to exercise moral or theological discernment over the act of possessing we have not simply allowed possession to become a neutral phenomenon, but by apparently giving possession *no* moral significance we have allowed it to acquire a power quite out of proportion to its actual reality. It now dominates us in the most frightening way. In actual fact, by effectively saying that possession – whether of material goods or psychological states – is something that the individual can or indeed should have in order to be complete, thus leaving it unthreatened by religious, moral or state control or guidance, we have actually unleashed a monstrosity. If something exists we now assume we have a right to possess it and use it, however difficult, dangerous or harmful such possession and use may be. This only reveals the extent to which we are controlled by a force or forces outside of ourselves – in this case the force of the need to possess. We are now, as people, almost totally preoccupied by questions of possession, ownership and control. Possession is a fascination. We have succumbed like rabbits to the stare of the snake.

I think this is why I found the conversation between the American sister of the Missionaries of Charity and the central heating engineer so revealing and important. For her there was no such fascination. Possession of a central heating system, even as a gift, was simply not a necessity. She said, quietly, "I don't think we need it". She had a simple disregard for possession. She was not occupied by the need to possess. It is this capacity for simple disregard that we need to recover.

Once we have recognized this then the debate can focus on the real issue – how to recover that simple disregard. What we should be talking about is how we might be set free from the need to possess, what is it that will liberate us? This is the central issue of our time, the resolution of which has personal and psychological, but also social and political, consequences, for the political is only the personal writ large. The argument of this book is that such a liberation can only be finally achieved by means of a recovery of greater confidence in the gift to us by God of the hidden journey on which we are all embarked. We have to recover our confidence that as human beings, however much we may think we lack, whether of material or psychological goods, we do not actually lack anything. We need to recover an interior confidence that we are full, that we have been created complete and that we need nothing more. We need to be able to look out upon the world without desire.

"I have five dollars"

We can illustrate this by returning once again to the creation narratives in the first two chapters of the book of Genesis. In the narrative of chapter two, a parallel account of creation, probably earlier than that in chapter one, Adam is taken by God and settled in the Garden of Eden, "to cultivate and take care of it". He is forbidden to eat of the tree of the knowledge of good and evil. When Eve is tempted by the snake she, "saw that the tree was good to eat and pleasing to the eyes, and that it was desirable for the knowledge that it could give". It is at this point that disaster occurs, for first of all Eve and then Adam find it impossible to accept that their original condition needs no more knowledge than what they have been given. They refuse to allow that some things are beyond them and they eat the apple. They were asked to be stewards of somebody else's knowledge but believe that the possession of ultimate knowledge is the better bet.

A contemporary Dominican writer, Simon Tugwell, in commenting on the creation narratives, points out that in Genesis chapter one – probably a later account – the writer states that God made man male and female, "in his own image and likeness". Tugwell goes on to say, "it is not simply a temptation to man to wish to be like God; he is meant to be like God. But he is meant to be like God by virtue of God's creating him that way, not by virtue of some human act of appropriation." Man has to accept likeness to God as gift, not grasp it for himself as his right.

The Genesis narratives then speak of the human condition as one which has lost its original innocence because of our desire to possess that which we have been given. Chapter two shows the primeval couple as grasping at complete knowledge rather than accepting their role as stewards. The account in chapter one is a parable of humanity's inability to accept its status as being made in the image of God as gift. The creation narratives are a parabolic comment on the inability of human beings to accept their apparently insecure position. They are unable to see that they do not need to possess what in fact they have been given. Simon Tugwell says, "The gesture of taking the fruit and eating it is an obvious symbol of man taking something into his own hand and storing it away safely inside himself. It is a symbol of that security of possession which has become such an obsessive concern of fallen man."[1] To be so obsessively concerned with the security of possession is to be fallen.

Jesus of Nazareth continues to remind us of the need to accept what we have in gladness rather than grasp at more or, even, hoard what we already have in little holes in the ground. It is not just in the parable of the talents that Jesus reveals his concern. The primary instance is the Sermon on the Mount and the Beatitudes in particular. "Blessed are the poor", or, as Matthew has it, "Blessed are the poor in spirit", is, in the first instance, a saying against greed. Worldly success is an obstacle to our capacity to turn and repent. But it also challenges our whole understanding of what "possession" means. This beatitude calls us to believe that we are happy because everything has already been given to us. The poverty we need is not so much the poverty of goods – although that is something to which we may be called and to which we must be ready to respond at any minute – but the poverty of an inner spirit which is always ready to live

with what is rather than with what can be appropri-
ated. We must live with the risk of loss and be glad
that this risk is there. We have to live in the poverty of
having nothing as our own because everything has
been given to us. This condition actually produces
such a degree of insecurity, especially when it is
accompanied by lack of belief in the unseen God who
created us in this condition, that we grasp at "possession" in order to alleviate our sense of desolation.
But, as Simon Tugwell says, "We must be prepared to
be dispossessed of all that we understand by life if we
would truly live."

The most complete answer to the materialism of the
present age is not, then, a simple denial of the urge to
possess. It is rather the inner realization of our own
freedom. In the spirit of this realization the need to
possess will drop away. Our inner freedom will allow
us to be with what we do not have. This confidence
derives above all from an interior confidence in the
hidden journey of love and trust upon which our being
is already embarked. Where we are being taken is
actually all right. The journey may be an unknown
one but it is a journey into and within the presence of
love. Surrender to this journey as a priority takes us
into the realm where possessions as such do not matter.
This does not mean that we will not actually own
things but it does mean that what we own will be
accepted as gift and relinquished or given back to the
giver whenever necessary. Such a capacity to live life
as gift, having embarked upon a silent and interior
journey of love and trust, is made almost impossible
by the contemporary predilection for living on the
surface, for moving from one island on the surface of

the painted sea to another, for collecting slides of the journey which we can then show to our friends rather than allowing ourselves to move in inner silence further towards our destination. True freedom from the need to possess derives from a confidence that this inner journey is sufficient and that it is a journey made in and to love.

This inner journey into the unknown darkness of love is the subject of the poems of St John of the Cross. One of the most striking is the poem entitled, "Song of the soul that is glad to know God by faith". Here St John speaks of the fountain's rushing glow, that river within which the spring is hidden but at which all heaven and earth find refreshment. This is the hidden spring of life within the soul which cries out, as the voice in Isaiah, "Ho, come to the waters, come and drink."

> Here to all creatures it is crying, hark
> That they should drink their fill though in the dark,
> For it is night.[2]

What often prevents either recognition of this way, or engagement upon it, in modern times, is the fear that this dark way is an end in itself, a cul-de-sac, even a form of masochism with dubious results. What is the point, it is argued, of depriving oneself of the joys and beauties of this world, the material benefits which have often been bought at a price, when the rewards are doubtful and intangible? Why follow the Amish when what we have won from our own efforts and our struggle with the forces of nature has given us a degree of comfort and a standard of living we did not have before? This, at least, was the form of the discussion which took place in the wake of our friend Jonathan's visit to America. It only too clearly reveals the conflicts in our hearts and at the heart of our society. These are conflicts between, on the one hand, acceptance, simplicity and recognition of the already given beauty of the earth and the hidden resources of the human person, and, on the other hand, struggle, achievement and domination over the creation and apparent control over the dark forces of the human personality. We so often prefer the latter because of the comfort that it appears to bring rather than the former because it involves saying no to the desire to possess. This requirement, the denial of the desire to possess, is rejected and castigated as a denial of God's gift of prosperity, or a denial of what we have achieved, or, more simply, as a religious fanaticism with unsure results. And it is true that fanatics have trod this path and muddied it for others, but no less than those who have trod the path of desire for control over the resources of the earth.

What needs to be made clear is that the path of denial is not an end in itself. It derives from a response to God himself. When his existence, his beauty and his love are understood to be primary, to be indeed all that we require, then the rest follows. We lose our need to grasp at other things. Acknowledgement of God's existence in the form of a dark river of love that flows, hidden and deep, within each person and from which not just each person but actually the whole creation drinks its fill, is an acknowledgement that will free us from the desire to possess. It will free us from the desire to possess the truths of religion, it will even free us, as Meister Eckhardt knew, from the desire to possess God. This acknowledgement will not only free us *from* attachments of various kinds, but will also free us *for* others and will enable us to live from the heart in simplicity and with a bias to the poor. It will enable us to live, if we will allow ourselves to accept it, with something of the life of God himself.

The great icon of this way in the twentieth century is the person whose life is the source and inspiration for the Little Brothers and Sisters of Jesus, Charles de Foucauld. A French aristocrat who began a military career but subsequently turned to exploration, he was one of the first Europeans to explore Morocco, dressed, interestingly enough, as a Jew. A dramatic conversion in Paris led to his entry into the religious life. After some years in a Trappist monastery in Syria he moved, with the permission of his religious superiors, and lived alongside a small community of nuns in Nazareth. Then, seeking further simplicity, he moved into the Sahara Desert where his hermitage was also a place of great friendship and of loving service. He translated the scriptures, prayed, hoped for others to join him, and befriended the people of the desert. One of the central emphases in his spirituality was that of "Nazareth". For him "Nazareth" was the symbol for the hidden life of the incarnate saviour. Jesus lived there, with the poor, himself poor, hidden from the eyes of the world, but also a living sign of the presence of God. De Foucauld followed this way of "Nazareth" himself, and it is still a central symbol in the spirituality of the Little Brothers and the Little Sisters of Jesus. This spirituality points the Church towards total simplicity as a means, indeed the supreme means, of the imitation of Christ in our day. Charles de Foucauld

says, "Let us stay with Him in the humble house of
Nazareth, working people who live by exercising a
humble trade, poor and lonely people who live disre-
garded . . . Jesus tells us to follow Him, so do it.
Share His life, His labours, His preoccupations, His
humiliations, His poverty . . ."[3] This way of identifi-
cation with the poorest of the poor continues today
in the life and work of the Little Brothers and Sisters
who live with the poor as signs of the presence of
Christ. That this way of life derives from an inner
freedom, an abandonment of the desire to possess,
can be seen from the writings of one of them, Carlo
Carretto. For him poverty was not a negation but a
beatitude. The silent, contemplative life, he believed,
that life of Nazareth which is so denied or repressed
by modern existence, is not the possession of a few
blessed souls, but is actually present in all of us and
needs to be released from its captivity. This is a great
surprise, because we feel so much that such a way of
life is only achieved by effort and then only by a few
brave (or foolhardy) souls, but it is latent within us
all, defeated by the spirit of the age. Not only can it
be released but it can also be completed and sustained
by action for and with the poorest. "Poverty", Carretto says, "is not a question of having or not having
money. Poverty is not material. It is a beatitude.
Blessed are the poor in spirit. It is a way of being,
thinking, loving . . ."[4]

In his dream, Thomas Merton finds himself standing
alone, trying to reach the party that he has been invited
to attend. Somebody, "a man of the town", tells him
that he can reach the party for a sum of money. He

has five dollars, more than that, in fact hundreds of dollars. But although what he has is great none of it in the end is sufficient. He has to let go and swim. Only then is he able to reach the furthermost shore.

"... a workaday fishing schooner"

In the end salvation is attained by the abandonment of any attempt to attain it. It is free gift. Any human achievement which is genuine derives from the same source, is a gift in response to gift, made because and in the joy that things are as they are – given by God. This does not mean to say that effort is not required. It is, and often in abundant measure. Nor does it mean that rational thought processes are put aside or lost in some rapturous vision. Often they are needed all the more. But salvation occurs when we recognize that it has been given to us already and that all of our efforts to lead the good life, our thinking or our striving to think the right thoughts, will not make it come any more quickly or any more surely than it has already. The gift is not ours to manipulate, nor is God ours to please. Nothing that we do will induce him to release his pleasure more or to delight in us more than he has or does already. He is gracious. He is pleasured by us. He does delight in what we are. He has always done so.

Salvation lies in recognizing these simple but difficult truths. Salvation lies in accepting that these things have been true from the beginning and will remain so until the end. But it is this acceptance that we have lost. Effectively we have become obsessed by achievement. We are both the victims and the perpetrators of a way of life which answers to our inner desire to achieve acceptable results. Society then reinforces this by rewarding enterprise. All of this is good. Enterprise and achievement do actually give pleasure and some fullness of being both to the individual and to the community; but they do not give pleasure or fullness of being when they come from the belief that meaning of life is to be found in enterprise and achievement. This would be to abandon ourselves to a view of human nature which, first of all, is reductionist – reducing human beings to being known only by what they can achieve. Moreover it is a hopelessly fatalistic view, condemning us to continuous production. It is not a view which can cope with handicap or loss or limitation. Nor is it a view which can delight in things as they are, for things as they are are never enough.

There are a number of such criticisms which can be made of this enterprise view of human nature, but perhaps the most substantial is that it is a view which actually misunderstands that which it claims to understand best, namely the very nature of work itself. Work, the theologians claim, contains much more than we know. It is a source of life in itself and it is because we have not acknowledged it as precisely that, but turned it into a *means* of life, that we have wrought havoc on ourselves and turned human beings into things rather than persons.

Let me explain what I mean. A few years ago a friend of mine was involved in a church-based project which attempted to find some basis for church work in Colleges of Further Education. These are the colleges which specialize in training people for industry and commerce and they take in large numbers of students, more than the universities and polytechnics combined, who follow what are popularly known as sandwich courses because they spend part of their time at work and part in the college. This means that the students are never present in the colleges for very long, and so the possibility of them forming some sort of community with fellow students is remote. It also means that for these students the hand- and eye-based skills are of the greatest importance. Pure intellect is not enough. It is also true that the Church, traditionally, has not taken these institutions very seriously, in spite of their very high student numbers. There has been little, if any, formal involvement by the Church in the life of these colleges in the way that there has been in the universities and polytechnics with their chaplaincy provision. Consequently these institutions, which are, in the end, amazingly important in the formation of the skilled worker upon whom so much in our society depends, contain a great deal of indifference and hostility towards the church. They contain no sustained official *theological* conversation on the nature of work.

It was into this apparently barren and indifferent world that my friend stepped. She was not entirely alone as she was supported by a consultative group. There were, or had been, a small number of similar experiments by the churches elsewhere. There was even a national officer who was trying to encourage and support these experiments. On the whole, however, it was a totally new sphere of work. But here great riches were to be found. Edwina found that in reality what Christians would describe – or perhaps, better, would describe if they were attentive enough – as theological language was alive and well. This "theological language" was out of touch with mainstream theological language, it did not use the same imagery or have the same degree of articulation, it was ignorant of all the technical terms which have informed Christian theology for hundreds of years and which common people have forgotten if they ever knew them, but it was there. What this language needed was somehow to be understood and linked in to the tradition. What the tradition needed was somehow to hear and to be refreshed by this language.

At the end of her time in this venture Edwina wrote a report for the churches.[1] In it she tried to articulate what she had heard. She said, "I listened to a plumber talking about metal. Metals fascinated him, and he stated the main source of his fascination: It's very deceptive. It looks manmade but it isn't. We find it, process it and make it into things, but we don't make the original metals. That's the mystery of it: you always have to remember, it's not manmade . . . In this non-church-going, non-Christian man there is a depth of sympathy towards his raw materials and a warmth of understanding, of mystery and givenness and a deep reverence in his approach to work. His insights are available to colleagues and students alike, in tiny snippets, the gentle comment or observation . . . Christians need to become aware of such people and learn from them and work with them: perhaps to offer a name to the mystery; more likely to explore and enjoy the mystery together."

". . . a workaday fishing schooner"

In her report Edwina went on to draw out some of the implications of what she saw and shared during her exploration of Further Education Colleges. Later on she says, "Two observations are possible from all this. The first, and very important, is the sense of joy, excitement, wonder and pleasure which clearly accompanies creative work. It would seem that people are instinctive creators. The second is the excitement which is evident when people create within limitations . . . when manual dexterity is challenged. Within all the given limitations, the quest is still there: to create, to do a job which can at the end be judged very good.'

Now clearly there are limits to this type of thinking. It should not be supposed, for example, that there is a great deal of beauty or creativity in every kind of work or in every kind of limited situation. Some work is nothing more than ugly and degrading. Some limited situations are designed to do nothing more than undermine the work being done. Nor should we erect a public policy on the view that all work *is* creative and all limits necessarily invigorating. Limits also destroy. But the substantive point remains, that work in itself is not an evil, but rather contains a mystery. If it is regarded purely as a means to an end then it becomes demonic. Work has a value in its own right. It belongs to the one who performs it, or maybe he or she even belongs to it. In any case it is part of the maker and the maker is part of it. What it is not is a commodity, necessarily saleable or contractable. In a real sense it is a gift. Work done may be recognized by financial or contractual means, it is never really purchased.

As I pondered on what Edwina was saying I realized that I had stumbled on something which was greater than one report or one person's musings upon it. I was already deep within an ongoing discussion, within the European theological and philosophical tradition, on the philosophy of work. I suspected that Calvin and Marx were there before me, particularly Marx. I decided to look some of it up. Yes, I was right, Marx had already laid his hand on all this. He reacted, as we all know, against the idealism of Hegel. What came first, said Marx, was the actual historical world in which men and women were set, not "ideas" about the world, or even "the idea" of God. "Ideas", and particularly "the idea of God" was, for Marx, the source of alienation and were kept alive by those in power in order to enable them to preserve their power. What was real was the world in which women and men existed. An absolutely basic feature of this human existence is the work which women and men perform. It is by this that they are constituted, in this that they are transformed. Marx says that it is a self-evident truth that "man must produce if he is not to die". In Marxist thinking, then, human beings actually become themselves by working.

It is this insight which forms the basis of Marx's protests when the very process by which men and women have discovered identity and by which they have been transformed is taken away from them by others and becomes a matter for barter or sale for less than its true value. This Marx calls the process of "objectification" – the process whereby what is essentially something else becomes a mere object, which can then be detached from its bearer and sold on the open market. The more common term for this is, of course, "the alienation of labour". For Marx labour cannot be alienated because it belongs to the worker as an inalienable part of his being. So Marx – and many others who have come after him – have charted with great persuasive power the process by which that which is so constitutive of human nature, namely the capacity to work, is taken away from him and becomes the source of his alienation. Arguments will continue amongst Marxist philosophers as to how inevitable that process is and what are the conditions by which it can be arrested; but the insight which survives is that it is capitalism which risks turning everything into a saleable commodity, including that which is most characteristic of human beings themselves, namely their labour. The implication is that this "labour" is originally, or is at root, something very precious which produces human identity. It is that which brings people into being. Nor is it necessarily – and this is clear from some of Marx's early writing – something which alienates. It need not be a matter of sale and barter, indeed it is to protect it from being such that resistance and, in the end, revolution is necessary. Resistance preserves human dignity as a working being, one who not only produces things but also himself in the process. The aim of resistance and revolution, whether or not this is the outcome, is to produce a society in which the essential nature of humanity does not automatically become the subject of alienation.

I have indulged in this little digression into Marxist thinking in order to demonstrate that musing about plumbers in Colleges of Further Education is not so very far from the mainstream of European philosophy. It also shows us that Marx, at least in his earlier years, had an amazingly positive view of work. He saw, in philosophical and economic terms, what my friend Edwina saw in religious terms, namely that work has a naturally humanizing quality. When this humanizing quality is taken away and trampled underfoot by the so-called progress of civilization, then protest must – and does – occur. The difficulty with Marxist thinking is that even though it appears to derive from a positive and humanistic basis, and there have been and continue to be a number of philosophers who would lay claim to "humanistic Marxism" as the true legacy of Marx himself, this has never been properly spelled out. Indeed it appears that it would have been alien to Marx's way of thinking to have done so. He was, after all is said and done, a historical materialist. To have relied upon a thoroughly worked out understanding of human nature would, in Marx's eyes, have risked relying upon an idealistic way of thinking. It would have been to erect a metaphysic when no metaphysic existed and was certainly not needed. It is at this point that Christians and Marxists have disagreed. Here my friend Edwina parts company from Karl Marx.

While Christians and Marxists have both fought against the alienation of human beings by the powers of this world, and need to be far more cognizant than they are of their common front in the struggle, their motivation is differently oriented. While Marxists have refused to elaborate any metaphysic of the human person, knowing only too well how such metaphysics can, in their turn, become the cause of oppression and fear, Christians have had no compunction in saying that human beings have an innate dignity given them by an exterior, transcendent personality. Because of

Christ humanity participates in divinity and this is why alienation by the powers of this world must be resisted. Whereas Marxists would say that such theology was in itself alienating, Christians would say that it is only with such beliefs that the struggle can be continued until the end. The quality of the end will, they would say, be determined by the philosophical means employed to support the struggle and without belief in God the struggle degenerates into mere politics and the true nature of humanity is not served.

But Edwina's report had set me going. I read other things about work and the Christian understanding of it. Some of it repelled me. What I did begin to feel was that the whole area was grossly undervalued. Everybody worked, whether in paid, regular employment or not, but nobody seemed to want to look at this universal activity in theological terms. Nobody seemed to want to understand it as it was before God. There was plenty of church literature about enabling the laity to participate in the work of the Church, giving the final death knell, I thought, to the chances of a prophetic ministry by Christians in their place of work and wrapping the clericalization of the laity in such fine words as "participatory ministry", but little, if any, especially in the Church of England, about a true theology of work. I shook my head sadly, once again, over the middle-class nature of the established church. Work was obviously something which other people did. The Methodists fared better, and I thought it was no surprise that my friend Edwina was a Methodist. But then I found a papal encyclical, *Laborem Exercens*, issued by Pope John Paul II in 1981.[2]

I read it carefully. What fascinated me were the

correspondences with Marxism, but also some sharp divergences at crucial points. The whole burden of the letter was that men and woman have a dignity in themselves – work is for people, not people for work. The Pope even takes on the anthropologists and names humanity *Homo Laborens* – "The Being who Works". It is work, he says, which distinguishes human beings from the rest of the created order, work which constitutes or defines us. This work derives from man's original character, given him at the creation, as participating in the likeness of God. "Man is the image of God partly through the mandate received from his creator to subdue . . . the earth. In carrying out this mandate, man, every human being, reflects the very action of the creator of the universe". So far so good, I thought, nothing new here; all good stuff, but not really very original. Then I came across a very important passage. The letter questions whether, in a technologically sophisticated age such as ours, human beings, although created in God's likeness, have not lost that likeness by allowing work to become a dominant force. The question is whether the relationship we have with technology has not come to mean that human beings are "the object" of technology, subservient to it, even at enmity with it, rather than still its master and able to use it as an ally in the pursuit of the kingdom. This was more like it, I thought.

Pope John Paul then goes on, in the central section of his letter, to talk of the importance of maintaining the priority of labour over capital. Whereas Marxism dehumanizes, capitalism does the same by giving capital priority over labour. Both Marxism and capitalism are forms of depersonalization. It is the Pope's intense

personalism which enables him to see that both collec-
tivist and materialist philosophies are deficient. Workers' rights, he says, must be respected – "economism",
as he calls it, is not a philosophy which must supplant
respect for the person. Human labour cannot be
considered solely according to its economic purpose.
Employers are called upon to ensure that their workers
are respected and understood as workers. The "indirect
employer", that is the multinational companies, also
have a duty to preserve the priority of labour over the
requirements of capital. The state also has duties, as it
pursues rational economic planning, to protect the
working person from the so-called inevitabilities of
market forces. Even better, I thought.

The final section of the encyclical speaks of the
importance of elaborating a "spirituality of work", and
of the duty of the Church to formulate such a spirituality in biblical terms. This spirituality will enable
women and men everywhere to see how they share in
the creative work of God and in the recreative work of
Christ on the cross. Human work is part of the
struggle for a new earth, "where justice dwells". The
Pope concludes, ". . . it is through man's labour that
not only 'the fruits of our activity' but also 'human
dignity, brotherhood and freedom' must increase on
earth". Amen, amen, I said to myself.

My immediate reaction was to say that if this is what
the Pope really thinks then it's a pity it doesn't come
across more clearly in his speeches, especially when he
goes to Latin America, where they really are fighting
for "human dignity, brotherhood and freedom". A
second, more intellectual reaction was to think that so
much of what he says in the encyclical is reminiscent

of the thinking of Teilhard de Chardin in *Le Milieu Divin*, where the great French thinker reflects on the contribution that each person's effort, however small, makes towards the consummation of all things in Christ. The irony is that Teilhard was condemned by the Vatican, silenced and exiled to China. Well, I thought, nothing's really wasted, but it is a pity that the Vatican finds it so difficult to rehabilitate publicly all those it silences.

But the principal value of the Pope's encyclical, I thought, was the profound personal value it discovered in work. Work, it seemed to be saying, contains a great deal more than we know. Our contemporary enterprise culture treats work as something with which we can obtain something else, something like a coin in our pocket rather than a deeply personal reality by means of which men and women can find identity. The Marxist and the Catholic traditions both, in their own ways and for their own reasons, recognize this. Work has its own intrinsic value, it is part of the way in which we come to wholeness, it has a life-giving quality about it. It is precisely because this is true that women and men should not be taken advantage of by their employers and their work exploited in order to produce wealth or power which is unshared. This was the whole impetus, I thought, both behind Marx and the encyclical. Both criticize capitalism for its sheer utilitarianism.

I thought, perhaps we ought to see work in a different light. Perhaps it would be best to describe work as a form of "response". After all, it is the central human response to being, it helps us realize and define our being, it is our response to recognizing that we are. It allows us to present ourselves to ourselves and to others. It allows identity to emerge. It provides the person with edges to the self and continues to allow him or her to develop the shape that his or her being has. It requires co-operation for its very existence and so produces community as well as identity. It is best recognized when it is allowed to emerge. It fails when it is forced or used purely as a means to an end. A utilitarian approach to work is one which completely undervalues what it really is. Above all work is response. It is response to that ancient beauty which derives from God and which informs all things and has informed them from the beginning. Allowed to rise from within, each new day, this response will itself produce beauty and create satisfaction and faith within the heart of each person.

Work is also a response which will revolt against its debasement. Work which is simply repetitive and boring, which undermines the dignity of the person, is hardly work at all. Against such work the human spirit revolts. It revolts because what it can be, what it has within itself to be, is denied. There is within each person an outpouring, a continuous response which, when frustrated, will build up pressure and anger and eventually burst. If our response in work is frustrated in one direction then human beings will find an outlet in another direction, in the creation of gardens or allotments or in home decoration or in art. So much of this is scorned by cognoscenti but in the end it is the response of those who can only respond in this way. Even with the most simple and limited of means human beings will work to respond to that invisible call of beauty which springs deep within them. Response to this beauty forms and creates who we are.

Work is not only a response, it is also an offering. The human person requires the space to offer his or herself, to lay out who they are as a form of self expression. Everybody will do this. What we know as "culture" is no more nor less than the fully worked out expression of who and what groups and nations are – it is an offering, a communal offering, of what people are and can do. The work we do is part of this. It is as much part of our culture as literature and music. When we are deprived of the opportunity of offering who we are through work then our spirit is diminished and dies. When the arts are understood to be totally disconnected from the world of work which they actually reflect and comment upon, then they become anaemic and introverted, precious and self-regarding.

Self-offering is central to human life. For Christians it is focused in prayer and the eucharist. These are those occasions when the ongoing self-offering of work is focused and concentrated and brought before God. They are concentrated periods of self-offering, personalized and interiorized in the case of prayer, ritualized and made public in the case of the eucharist. There are different levels and different styles of prayer but the essential characteristic of true prayer is this sense of offering, of laying out, of presenting to and for God who we are and what we can do. Then in the light which he sheds upon it we know what it is in our offering that constitutes life and what it is that has to be shed or abandoned. Prayer, then, is a focusing, a deliberate concentration of what we are, of our work and its source of energy, and a presentation of it before God. It is a self-offering. Work is simply the expanded, daily self-offering in practical terms, an expanded and enlarged version of what happens, in personal, miniature terms, as it were, within the span of prayer.

The eucharist is the public offering of our lives and our work in the ritualized framework given us by Christ and the Church. It is a recollection of what we have been, a presentation of our self-memorizing and an offering of that in the light of the offering of Christ in his life and death. As we offer ourselves in union with his self-offering on Calvary then who and what we are is taken, stripped, purified and renewed by the love and mercy of God and given back to us restored and enlivened. The bread and wine of the eucharist contain, as they are offered, all that we have been doing up to that point. As the bread is offered it participates in the ongoing offering of Christ, is broken and poured with him but is given back to us transformed, just as he was given back to his disciples at the resurrection. Work is our self-offering, prayer and the eucharist are the action by which that self-offering is focused and brought into the life of God. It is then purified and transformed, given back to us shot through with the life of God himself, given back to us in a way in which we can see what parts of it we need and what parts we do not need, given back to us as food which then carries us a day's march further on our journey.

The social implication of all this is, of course, that we should allow human beings the opportunity to offer themselves in work. It means that to deliberately deprive somebody of work is an action which deprives them of the chance to offer the very core of their being into existence. It also means that the work which we provide must be such as to enable that offering to take place. "Mere work" is not enough. It has to be such that human beings feel able to offer through it who and what they are. Work has to be valued for its hidden, inner, sacramental qualities. Social and economic policies which do not do this only fail the truth, they fail the truth of what we are as human beings as well as the truth about work itself. Such policies only store up problems for themselves until such time as they are adjusted to take account of these hidden realities.

As I reflected on all this I began to realize that none of it was new or original. It is a way of seeing things that flourishes, for example, in the writings of Eric Gill, the carver and stonemason who flourished at the turn of the century. Gill himself was inspired by Ruskin and Carlyle, the visionaries of the Victorian era. These men agreed – in the face of the dehumanizing effects of the industrial revolution – that work must be ennobling. Work which did not allow the inner spirit of human beings to flourish could not be called work as such. Individual creativity, Gill would maintain, is not simply the preserve of the artist. It also belongs to the farmer in his fields and to the bricklayer laying bricks. Gill would quote with approval the saying of the Indian writer Coomaraswamy, "The artist is not a special kind of man but every man is a special kind of artist." Another Victorian who held similar views was William Morris, the socialist writer and designer. For Morris work was creative and part of the work of the creator God.

Industrialization, just as much as the pursuit of the leisure state, undermined and destroyed this creative potential in human beings. Morris pre-empted the Pope's encyclical when he said, a hundred years before, ". . . for what is an artist but a workman who is determined that, whatever else happens, his work shall be excellent".

And so I found myself coming full circle, back to my friend Edwina and her plumber who was so fascinated by metal and the gift that it contained, who recognized something of the inner mystery of the work that he did, even though he could give no name to that mystery. William Morris and Eric Gill would have been proud of him, I thought. Let alone the Pope! For work is part of our hidden journey. Its source is hidden from our eyes. It is only when we allow work to flow from this hidden inner source that it becomes real and allows us to become who we really are. When it derives from our desire for gain or power, when it loses its own intrinsic qualities and is forced into a utilitarian mould which insists on saying that it must be "for" some visible and realizable gain, then it ceases to flow from this inner source and has been diverted to irrigate some little project of our own. Then it will cease to feed and sustain us. We must continue to allow it to come from we know not where and to take us to we know not where.

This is precisely why, in his dream, Thomas Merton failed to launch the boat. The boat is a workaday schooner. He spends a long time trying to push it out by means of his own efforts. He thinks he can possess and sail it to the other side. He thinks work is his, that it will get him somewhere. His pushing symbolizes his refusal to accept the divine origin of work. In the end he has to rely on grace, so he lets go and swims.

". . . Christian social action, on the contrary, conceives man's work itself as a *spiritual* reality, or rather it envisages those conditions under which man's work can *recover* a certain spiritual and holy quality, so that it becomes for man a source of spiritual renewal, as well as material livelihood."

"Whatever may be the explanation, I am struck and troubled by the fact that if the Jews were called out of Egypt, out of peace into anguish, it was because God did not will that His People should merely live productive, quiet, joyous and expansive lives."[3]

"... two pieces of buttered white bread"

I was once appointed vicar of a parish which celebrated the eucharist with a whole loaf and a bottle of home-made wine. All this sounded good, a clear rejection of an over-emphasis on meaningless ritual and an offering of the "real" bread and wine of the people. "Well", I thought, "at least the eucharist is central here and they are trying to bring it all to life!" Before very long, however, I found myself struggling with things I knew I did not like without being able to articulate very clearly why. It was partly the loaf, which arrived at the altar on a wooden bread board with a bread knife. I had to cut away the crust and then slice enough for those who were there – all during the remaining verses of the offertory hymn and under full gaze of the congregation. It was not just the embarrassment, it was the fact that it was all supposed to be so meaning-ful. I felt I was playing at liturgy. The wine was another matter. It being home-made presented me with no problems – what I found difficult was that it was so very seldom grape wine. It was more often rhubarb or elderflower. But how could I change it without offending the sensibilities of those who proudly offered their bottled workmanship week after week? After an internal tussle between the rival claims of local feelings and the universal practice of the Church I approached one of the churchwardens and asked that we use grape wine. This we did, although I think people were surprised and not a little suspicious of what this might portend.

A similar struggle – both internal to me and external within the congregation – occurred over the robes. We used a set of dowdy grey-brown albs which were supposed to reproduce, I was told, the robes worn by the brothers in the monastic community of Taizé. Now I was an admirer of the Taizé brothers, but could find very little in these albs to resemble that awe-inspiring place. We looked as if we were wearing dressing gowns. From the outset I resisted being muffled up in something quite so drab and wore white, eventually persuading the people that everybody at the altar should be in white.

I was puzzled at the situation because in principle I was in favour of liturgical reform. I had begun my ministry by introducing new liturgies to the people and had continued to do it ever since. Why did I now find myself apparently going back on the progress that had been made? Why was I prepared to risk the wrath of a group of people with whom I had – at first sight – so much in common? In the end it began to come clear to me, although whether it has ever come clear to my congregation I shall probably never know. What I was feeling was that by over-emphasis on such everyday forms of liturgical expression we risked losing our sense of beauty, mystery and transcendence in worship. God is certainly involved in our everyday life, but he is also greater than all that we know and cannot be reduced to that which we know. Moreover the human soul requires contact with beauty and with mystery in order to remain uplifted, inspired and so human. Here in place of beauty we had the banal. In place of mystery we had the commonplace. In place of the transcendent we had what we had every day of the week. And like so many of the words and phrases of the new liturgies the form was also radically unpoetic. Moreover it was all so deliberate, the symbolism so heavily meaningful that at times it became funny, especially if you managed to cut yourself when slicing bread at the altar or found yourself tasting parsnip when you had expected grape! It risked becoming a sort of game, with its own rules, quite disconnected from the whole question of God or what it meant to be the Church.

Changing it all was a sobering experience. It made me think out at some length what I really thought worship was all about, why we did it and what we expected from it. In particular it made me realize just how easy it was for the liturgy to become captive to the spirit of the times – in this case the spirit of the bourgeois world of which I was so inextricably a part. I came to know just how much we all needed to be placed at least within reach of the invisible in order to put our souls within reach of being changed. Without that availability I felt we would never rise above an endless round of "church life", which was simply another form of human association with nothing in it to differentiate it from any other human association. We would all be, if we were not careful, one-dimensional. We were not called to play at middle-class church life, we were called to turn and turn and turn again.

During all the discussions that went on at this time I was reminded of a phrase, which I think comes from John Wesley, which says that the eucharist is "a missionary ordinance". It is a sign of the Kingdom and so a call to repentance and grace. Now it was not in my mind even to begin to suggest that a celebration of the eucharist with bread and home-made wine while wearing dressing gowns did not lead to repentance. What I was concerned to do was to ensure that the outward form of the sacrament expressed its inward reality and to affirm that just as that inward reality could be obscured by old-fashioned high-church ritual, so also it could be obscured by fashion, endless experiment, invented symbolism and banality.

And so I was brought face to face with the question, "What does it all mean?", and found myself, one Maundy Thursday, turning to St John's Gospel for an answer. And there I found another strange thing. St John gives no account of the final meal that Jesus shared with his disciples which can in any way be described as the beginnings of the eucharist – at least nothing which resembles the meal as it is recounted in the other Gospels. There is no mention of the bread and wine. There are no words, "This is my body, this is my blood." There is no indication of what sort of meal it was, no implicit connections with the ongoing ritual of the Jewish people. The most important thing which happens is that Jesus washes the disciples' feet. This is given a central place. When it is finished Jesus says to them, "I give you a new commandment, love one another." There is no question of St John displacing or undervaluing the significance of the eucharist. Any perusal of the Gospel shows that for him the eucharist is central. Jesus is "the bread from heaven" in a way which the other evangelists have not begun to grasp. Chapter six of the Gospel is more heavily eucharistic than any account of the Last Supper in Matthew, Mark or Luke. What he seems to be saying is that if you are looking for the inner meaning of the eucharist then you will find it not so much in the bread and the wine, although those remain central, but in the washing of feet. That act contains the inner, hidden meaning of the eucharistic feast. The meaning of the sacrament is contained in service of each other, in the washing away of the dust and dirt of life in acts of mutual dedication. Perhaps the kernel is found in the dialogue with Peter who resists the washing, but is asked to accept, to let go and let be, to allow God to come to rest in him. Just as God comes to rest in us so we should come to rest in each other.

As I pondered I remembered a sermon I had heard as a young curate. I remembered being disturbed when the visiting preacher, an industrial chaplain who was speaking of the relationship between the world of the sacraments and the world of work, said that the eucharist was "nothing to do with bits of bread and cups of wine". I now know more what he meant. The eucharist is a focus for the renewal of trust between ourselves and what we are given by God. As we receive the eucharistic elements we open ourselves to love and to the reception of love. In the bread and the wine the love of God, as known through Jesus Christ, is poured into us. As we receive the ordinary we are given the extraordinary. But merely receiving the bread and the wine as gifts of and from the mystery of God is only the beginning. These gifts are signs that all is gift. These particular signs indicate that all is sign, that nothing is exempt or empty. And if we cannot receive each other and minister to each other as gift and sign then we have not been open to God in the sacramental action. There is a continuum between the way in which we minister the sacraments to each other and the way in which we minister ourselves to each other. If we minister to each other in depth and see and receive each other as signs and gifts of God, then we will, I believe, be doing the eucharist with each other whether or not there are "bits of bread and cups of wine" passing between us. Moreover if we do minister to each other in depth and see and receive each other as signs of the mysterious presence of God the unknown lover, then we will, as time goes on, find ourselves wanting to share with one another more explicit signs of that mysterious presence, and the eucharist will arise naturally between us. Conversely, if we celebrate the eucharist joyfully and gladly as the sign of God's mysterious presence amongst us, accepting that it is genuinely a gift from God, then we will, I believe, find ourselves naturally celebrating *each other* as gifts and valuing each other as bearers of good news. People will then become gift rather than threat.

The net result of my reflections was a heightened awareness of both the mystery of the eucharist and of the mystery of human persons. I did not find myself wanting to return to bread boards or home-made wine, although I suspect that without them I might not have reached the point I did. At least they catapulted me into deeper reflection. Instead I found myself with a much deeper reverence for the hidden presence of the divine in the ordinary, and wanting to celebrate that presence liturgically in as rich and as real a manner as possible. The old liturgical mannerisms would not do, but the new, invented ways were not rich or strong enough either. We needed to find a way of celebrating that would support and offer all that we find as gift and mystery in life. Tragedy, loss, death, overwhelming joy, freedom, pain, passion, love – all these things and so many more had to find their place in our celebrations, and these things are mysterious, strange gifts from outside ourselves. To reduce the liturgy to what we could understand, therefore, was not only to do it a disservice, it was also to sell ourselves short, to underestimate the place of gift and mystery as actual components of what it means to be human.

And so I found myself in the position of wanting to celebrate the eucharist differently. I wanted to offer it with a greater intensity, more slowly, with greater emotional openness, with far greater simplicity but with even more dignity and stillness than ever the old liturgies could contain. I wanted silence rather than continuous activity. I wanted a greater depth. I knew that the fuss and bother of the "Parish Communion" somehow could not carry all that we wanted to say. I wanted our worship to be tuned to the music of this deep, still, hidden journey which I felt we were all making but which somehow the Church and church life continually seemed to miss. What we really were before God was not being offered. What was being offered was good enough – people who came said it was a revelation – but somehow it did not speak at sufficient depth.

121

I was blessed at the time with a sensitive curate, who knew all this instinctively better than I did. He had an innate liturgical sense and knew how people needed, as he said, to drink at the waters of life in worship. And gradually, together, we found a way of offering the eucharist which began to do the things we felt we needed to do. It expressed something of the mystery of what we were about. We began to celebrate the eucharist on a Sunday evening. We used icons with lots of candles and kept the church quiet and dark. We left a lot of silence in the service, interspersed with simple chants from Taizé and Iona, beautifully sung by a young medical student. We did not preach, but left the service to speak for itself. We encouraged people to come and sit or kneel around the altar rather than always hiding behind pews. We dispensed with acolytes but involved people in the readings and the prayers as much as possible. In this way, gradually, we began to express with our bodies and our voices something of the hidden journey of worship and praise which our souls were engaged upon but which the more formal worship of the church somehow failed to express – indeed, even left alienated at the end of the day.

Several things happened when we did this. Firstly we realized that worship was about beauty and the expression of beauty rather than about "liturgy" and "the tradition of the Church". Surely, what we were doing was clearly part of the liturgical tradition of Christendom, but the focus had shifted. Whereas for the last twenty years the Church had been preoccupied with "the liturgical movement" such that this "movement" had replaced what liturgy is really for, we were now clearly expressing – with the assistance of the reforms the liturgical movement had brought us – something of our sense of the beauty and majesty of God, something of our sense of penitence at our misuse of this beauty and something of our deep sense that this beauty was not so much outside ourselves but deeply implanted within us and the world in which we lived. This beauty was working its good work in us and this was being acknowledged and expressed so that it might bear fruit. We had come through to where we needed to be. We were free to worship rather than – as had been the case when I arrived – play around with bread boards and so feel that we were part of the "advanced" or "progressive" section of the Church. A little perception would demonstrate that none of the gains of the movement for reform were lost – it was plainly a people's eucharist – but nor had we given ourselves over to stupid play acting. Spending an hour on Sunday thinking about God in a progressive manner was no substitute for worship.

The second thing that happened was that we found ourselves more deeply united with Christians of other traditions. We found that our eucharist was attended by Methodists and Catholics as well as Anglicans. We found ourselves more easily at home when we went to their services, whether it was the Catholic eucharist with its deeply incarnational spirit or the Methodist service with its strong strand of musical praise. Links between us all grew and were rooted not just in friendship but in common devotion.

The third thing that happened was that people came to our liturgy who were not, or who had not been, part of our regular congregation and who had, perhaps, found themselves ill at ease with what the churches were offering. Some of them were involved in "political" activity – not so much party politics but rather the search for justice and change in society. They were people who were working in areas of social conflict, trying to listen to what was happening to those who were not part of a successful society. They did not come often, nor did they come in great numbers, but every now and again they were there, searching for restoration, new energy, forgiveness, the life of God.

Nor should anyone imagine that any of this happened easily or that we had some blinding vision about it. Much of what happened and where we were being led I can only see with hindsight. At the time it was sometimes fraught, caught up in all the petty feelings that we are naturally heir to. We argued about the music, we felt suspicious of what other people really wanted, we sometimes found it very difficult to move into new attitudes. But in the end something came of it.

I have recounted all this at some length partly because I felt it was worth recounting. It is part of the history of the Church in our day. It is certainly not unique by any means, but the story might encourage others who are struggling for meaning in the eucharist. More importantly I have recounted it because it was an experience of how a group of people tried to relate the external worship of the Church to their own hidden journey. In the end we knew that each of us was embarked upon a hidden journey with God and to God. We knew also that somehow we wanted this journey to be expressed in our worship – we wanted what we said in church to be part of what was actually going on within us. We knew that the tradition of the Church should relate to our hidden selves. We knew it said it related, that it yearned, as it were to relate more closely, but our experience of this relationship was sporadic and broken.

Some people, faced with this situation, begin to mistrust their own hidden selves. They feel that what is going on within them, when they come face to face with it, is not what the Church says it should be – it is not good enough or not holy enough and so they abandon their hidden selves and take on the "spiritual" life which they feel the Church wants them to have. They go on retreat, they pray in a special way, they go to confession for things they have been told are wrong and, generally speaking, adopt a false spiritual life. They worship in the way the Church tells them to worship. Sensible clergy are continually trying to save people from the effects of a *false* spirituality and finding themselves castigated for being unspiritual or political! Others move in a different direction and follow their own way, leaving the Church to work itself out. This might be initially more honest, but in the end the hidden life finds it has no expression. It wanders, like an undead soul, looking for a home but cannot find one. One of two or three things then happens. This undead soul, the spiritual life without a home, either lies hidden in the soul continually dying, leaving the owner of this spirit saddened and even bitter about the Church; or it lapses into romantic sentimentalism, linking God with sunsets or tinsel at Christmas; or, worse, it turns to the occult and finds an expression in tarot cards or ouija boards or black magic. The task of the Church is to give a home to the undead, to allow them to come to life, to provide expression for the hidden journey on which we are all embarked, to provide a haven for the soul.

The eucharist is essentially the place where this happens – or at least ought to happen. The kernel of its meaning is found in the response of Peter when Jesus comes to wash his feet. At first he draws back, but then, when faced with the questioning of his Lord, lets go and comes forward. Each of us, at the eucharist, is faced with that question. It is the question of whether we will trust the unseen, whether we will embark upon our hidden journey, whether we will set out into the darkness believing it to be love alone. The eucharist is the place where that question is asked and answered as nowhere else. The invitation to communion contains the interrogation of Peter by Jesus. Our response must also contain his cry, "Not just my feet, but also my hands and my head!" The eucharist is the gateway to trust, it is the focus for our commitment to the journey that we are called upon to make, it is the entry point into the hidden and mysterious journey into the unknown who is God. Refusal of the eucharist is a refusal of what is necessary to us as human beings, it is a refusal of what we were made for. Such a refusal leaves us stranded, unable to proceed. Such a refusal leaves us on the bank of the waters of life perpetually unable to plunge in and be carried to our destiny. Such a refusal leaves us holding our inner life in our hands with nowhere to put it, no means by which it can live but no ability to put it down safely – we are left with sentimentalism or black magic, and both can so easily lead to violence.

This kernel of meaning has been obscured because

of the Church's debates about the presence of Christ in the sacrament. These debates have all been couched in terms which give a static quality to the presence of Christ, terms which rely more on the correct doctrinal expression than on anything else. Even in the present climate we risk carrying on the debate in the same way. Christ's presence in the eucharist is a dynamic one, real but active, calling us to repentance and commitment. It is a presence which has the same dynamic as any other human presence – one which calls us to trust and love – but is a presence which is not local or restricted. It calls us into relationship with Christ and through him with God, and from there with every other person and with the whole created order. It calls us to trust that the truth about things is the mystery of love, that death and disaster, although present and although necessary, are not the final word.

Once again it is the poets who understand all this clearly. The classic expression of it is to be found in George Herbert's poem, "Love":

> Love bade me welcome; yet my soul drew back,
>   Guilty of dust and sin.

Herbert beautifully expresses the movement from fear and apprehension to trust, drawn out by love, and sets this in the context of the eucharistic feast.

> "You must sit down", says Love, "and taste my
>   meat."
> So I did sit and eat.

More recently the same movement has been expressed in a dramatic poem by Kathleen Raine, "Northumbrian Sequence". In one section of the poem the

speaker, who is perhaps the Virgin Mary, speaks of her
fear at the raging of the night but knows that she must
open herself to it, for it is gift, the gift of God to her.

> Fearful is my virgin heart
> And frail my virgin form,
> And must I then take pity on
> The raging of the storm
> That rose up from the great abyss
> Before the earth was made,
> That pours the stars in cataracts
> And shakes this violent world?
>
> Let in the fire,
> Let in the power,
> Let in the invading might.
>
> Gentle must my fingers be
> And pitiful my heart
> Since I must bind in human form
> A living power so great,
> A living impulse great and wild
> That cries about my house
> With all the violence of desire
> Desiring this my peace . . .
>
> Let in the wound,
> Let in the pain,
> Let in your child tonight.[1]

These last limes could be Christ's words to Peter at
the Last Supper. In any case they are words which
echo and re-echo through the history of the Church,
for they express so clearly what it is that we are called

to do. The mystery is that the child we are called to let in to our lives is not just Christ, it is also ourselves.

At the end of his dream Thomas Merton arrives at the house on the further shore. There he knows that he will be greeted by a child. Those who know the story of Merton's life will know that he led a lonely childhood, that his mother died when he was very young and his father while he was still at school. He also fathered a child while he was an undergraduate at Cambridge. All this combines in the arrival of the Christ Child in his dream who comes to him in mercy and forgiveness to greet him at his homecoming.

"I know the Child will come, and he comes. The Child comes and smiles. It is the smile of a Great One, hidden. He gives to me, in simplicity, two pieces of buttered white bread, the ritual and hieratic meal given to all who come to stay."

"... then I know that I must strike out and swim"

In the popular imagination prayer is probably understood in a very similar way to Latin. Latin is a language which people used to speak, apparently all over Europe, but nobody speaks it any more except for a few people in universities and places like that. It's certainly of no use to ordinary people unless they want to be able to decipher the inscriptions on tombs which they see in churchyards or cathedrals or, of course, if they want to spend their lives reading old manuscripts. It might help to understand the past but normal human beings don't use it any more. They don't need it in order to be what everybody wants to be – in communication. It's more important nowadays to learn a computer language like Basic or Cobol than to learn Latin. The ordinary run of secular society understands prayer in the same way. It's a language that people used to speak in the days when everybody was supposed to be religious, but nowadays we've found we can do without it. People live quite happy lives, apparently, without praying. Some people still pray – in monasteries and churches – but they are peripheral to the modern human consciousness. They seem to enjoy it and, so long as it doesn't do anybody any harm, there's no reason why they shouldn't. If we suddenly find out that it actually works then there might be some point in doing it, but so far there's no proof. So it's a dead language.

Obviously, from the religious point of view, such an attitude begs a few questions. This popular view assumes that some vital questions have been answered in a particular way. The first of these is the question of the existence and nature of God. Saying prayers normally assumes, even in a vague kind of way, both that God is and that his nature is such not just that he *may* be spoken with, but that he actually *wants* to be spoken with. The contemporary attitude has accepted that God does not exist or at least he does not exist in such a way as to be able or willing to communicate with humanity. Secondly, the contemporary attitude begs the question about human nature. Prayer may not be the most favourite pastime of modern men and women but does that actually make it unnecessary? May it not still be a *human* pastime? However true it may be that the modern condition does without prayer how true is it that the modern condition is actually *the* human condition? The contemporary assumption is that what we are now is what we actually are. The third question that is begged by the modern condition is that of the utility of prayer. It assumes that prayer should work, that being useful to us in particular ways is part, or at least a pretty essential part, of its function. Once that function has been disproved or overtaken by other, more powerful mechanisms then prayer or the spiritual life becomes unnecessary, a hobby for those who like that sort of thing. The question is, however, whether prayer should be regarded as something useful, which "works" to bring benefits to its practitioners. Is that all that prayer is? Or is it that we just cannot see that it does bring benefits?

The theological world – that is preachers, church leaders, clergy and theologians of all sorts – has tackled each of these questions in turn in order to try to bring us back to a living understanding of prayer. All this only shows, by the way, why the question of prayer is so important and so central. The way in which we understand and talk about prayer is bound together with the way we understand and talk about a number of central features of Christian belief. This list is not exhaustive, but it does include, notably, our understanding of God, our conception of the human person and the whole question of the usefulness or "the point" of faith. The current interest in spirituality arises from the realization that this is true and from a quest – under that general term "spirituality" – to bring all these features together in a way which makes sense. In other words spirituality is a quest for an integrative approach to the whole of Christian believing. Talk about spirituality is talk about a "way of seeing things" which sees things whole. But all that apart, much of contemporary Christian writing revolves around various attempts to bring the Christian way alive by tackling one or other of these three questions. These questions are, first, "How can we talk about God in such a way as to set people free to want to relate to him in prayer?"; second, "How can we talk about the human person in such a way as to show that prayer is natural?"; and, third, "How can we talk about prayer in such a way as to allow people to see that doing it is to their advantage?"

These are the questions we are left with after secularization has done its work on the life of prayer. The older, more authoritarian answers no longer serve. It is no longer enough simply to tell people that this is what they have to do as Christians. It is no longer enough to declare that Christ, or the Church or scripture makes this demand upon us. Nor is it enough simply to tell people that prayer works. This, to my mind, is the difficulty with trying to come at the matter through the third of the questions outlined above, that is the question about what is the point of it all. The abandonment of prayer by this generation because they have lost faith in whether it works is, I am sure, an entirely creative step forward. Prayer is not magic, nor can it be reduced to being an act of persuasion, even if the goods one is persuading the Almighty to give one are manifestly good. We might well be asking for the right things but it is an act of hubris for us to assume that we have the right to name what is good and to claim it for ourselves. In the end only God knows what is good, and our sight is partial. We can only guess at what we need for our final good and what we actually need may be quite other, indeed in the long run it may even be the opposite to what we are asking for today.

Moreover, talking about prayer as if it has to be something which works or does not work, or which is useful for us or not useful, is to allow our understanding of prayer to be totally dependent upon the utilitarian spirit of the age. Prayer cannot be reduced to being a form of "spiritual materialism" by which we obtain spiritual goods in the deception that amassing spiritual goods is somehow acceptable whereas the amassing of material goods is not. All goods are goods and all goods, perhaps even especially the religious sort, are obstacles to the activity of grace in our lives. To abandon prayer because it does not give you what you want is a step forward in the religious life because it sets you free to believe in a God who is not circumscribed by your own desires. In the end we have to come through to accepting that there is a "uselessness" about prayer. Prayer is something which we do because it is there for us to do. It is to do with God, with our acceptance in faithfulness of who he is; it is to do with the uselessness of adoration and love.[1] Let us take an analogy from human relationships for a moment. I do not love my wife, nor other people their loved ones, because it is useful to do so. We love, well, because ... We do not always know why, and the surest road to the breakdown of a human relationship is to announce to the other person that he or she is unable to give you what you want. If it so happens that my wife does give me what I both want and need (which, thankfully, she does) that is only finally so because of the mystery of love and is, in the end, more a matter for joy and thanksgiving than anything else. In utilitarian terms our love may well be a pretty useless sort of affair, but we, I suspect in common with most married people, are quite happy about that.

Nor, strangely enough, does any of this mean that we should not ask for things in prayer. Asking is a natural and basic part of any serious prayer life. But once the utilitarian motive for prayer is removed then we are set free to ask within a relationship which is not grounded in acquisitiveness. Once again the human analogy clarifies. Within a relationship of love people naturally ask each other to give. Even when the answer is "No", the relationship grows in strength because now the one asking knows what it is that he or she can ask for and be given freely and knows more surely what it is that he or she really needs. The next time asking occurs it stems from a greater clarity and self-knowledge which itself strengthens the bond of love. By listening to the response of its parents to its demands a child comes to know that it is loved and what it means to be itself. Its identity is fashioned by acceptance of the response. Its self-love and love for its parents are defined and strengthened both in the acceptance and in the denial of the demands it makes. The child comes to know in what its own final good consists by listening to the response father and mother make to its requests; but the relationship founders when the child does not or cannot learn, when the relationship is entirely dependent upon asking for and being given perceived wants. So too in the invisible life before God. We ask because we are first loved and love in response.

Meanwhile a lot of strides have been made towards finding a way of talking about God so that people are set free to want to relate to him in prayer. This is the first of the questions given to those who wish to keep the religious way alive in our secular age. Strides have been made because it is now possible to talk about God using human analogies in a way it was not while the theological influence of Karl Barth reigned supreme. We know that these analogies are just that, analogies and no more, but we are content, indeed more than content, to use them. In particular we are becoming more at ease, thank goodness, with more feminine images of God, thus linking ourselves more clearly with an earlier theological age when these images were more commonplace and had not been displaced by the excessively masculine images brought in by the so-called "rationalism" of the Enlightenment.

Our images of God have become more human in parallel, it seems, with the way in which we have regained confidence in our ability to talk about Jesus of Nazareth. In previous years it was felt, particularly by those who had fallen under the influence of Rudolf Bultmann, that not very much could be said about Jesus and even what could be said was, we were warned, deeply flawed by the distance of our perspective. Nor, by any means, were all the results of this period in the history of exegesis entirely negative. Not all of the lessons which we needed to learn have been learned. But it is none the less true that we have now lost a total silence about Jesus in the face of what appeared to be the evidence. Even if we are only content with what has been called "The Shadow of the Galilean"[2] then at least we are able to see where some of the outlines of the shadow fall. Furthermore we are no longer quite so nervous about the Holy Spirit. It is certainly true that we should remain nervous, especially in the face of some of the very divisive theology that has been thrown up in our day; but it is also true that theologians of all persuasions now recognize the need for there to be a properly balanced pneumatology as the basis of any exposition of the Christian position.

But whereas all of this is true, and the God of whom

we speak is now both more accessible and more warmly delineated than almost at any time for the last fifty years, so that it should now be possible to encourage people to speak to her (or him, whichever you choose) without fear, we have still not arrived at the position where large numbers of people are taking up the chances the theologians are striving to offer them. People don't seem to be rushing to church in greater numbers than they were before we began to talk about God using, for example, female imagery; however important it was that for reasons connected with the internal logic of our discourse, we did so. However pretty the girl is you have still got to find within yourself the courage and the impetus to speak to her. This is why in the long run the most important question we face in the attempt to rehabilitate the religious life is the second of those bequeathed to us by our secular age, that is the question about the human person.

The question remains, "How can we talk about the human person in such a way as to show that prayer is natural?" Whereas it has been and will remain important to respond clearly to the contemporary question about whether prayer "works" – and I have already indicated that I think the best response to this question is to demonstrate how the question itself is wrongly placed – and whereas it has been and will remain important to continue to find ways of talking about God which are accessible to our partners in the conversation – otherwise we shall be left talking to ourselves – in the long run the most important task is to restore people's confidence in their own hidden life. It is confidence in this that has been destroyed by a generation of false psychologism which has misled people into believing that their inner life is difficult or dangerous. It is confidence in this that has been destroyed by too great a trust in the capacity of "mind" to solve all of our problems. We are left with a generation which is starved of awareness of its own hidden existence, starved of careful direction about the nature of this life and so either petrified to enter into dialogue with it – so perpetuating male dominant roles and excessive reliance upon outward form – or so enamoured of the discovery that this hidden side to their personalities exists that they rush into it headlong and so lose themselves immediately in the uncharted waters of the occult or schools of transcendental awareness. The people of Europe and the West are faced with the most enormous sense of loss and inner deprivation. They feel that they are in a wilderness. The wilderness is a theological one but, more importanly, it is a wilderness within. They have no confidence that what they are is of any worth or beauty. All has been sacrificed to the external goals of comfort and success. The primary task of the churches is to restore that confidence in the intrinsic worth of the person. We have to recover our sense of delight, delight in God but also delight in the self.[3] The burden of these pages is that this sense of delight is one which must reach far deeper and must touch our most hidden areas. The hidden journey upon which we are all embarked is not one which will take us into nothingness, but one which will take us, if we would only let it, into the darkness of God. He is God of all that is, both seen and unseen. We have to restore the confidence of humanity in its hidden existence, to show

how this hidden existence is, in the end, of God. In this way people will be able to recover their own sense of inner coherence and unity, thus reducing the necessity of relying upon conflict with others as the only means we have left of resolving our tensions. In one of his journals Brother Roger of Taizé records his impressions on returning to Taizé from Asia. He says, ". . . in the northern hemisphere there is a thirst for God, and it is even becoming more intense. No, our life in Europe has nothing derisory about it. But, seen from Asia, it seemed clearer than ever that the northern hemisphere has vast tracts of spiritual deserts stretching across it. These wastes are the haunts of boredom, disenchantment and a diffuse doubt that leads to scepticism."[4] It is this thirst in the desert of our civilization that must be answered.

Prayer is an opening up of and to the interior self, an opening up so that we can acknowledge and own this self and then place it before God. It is an outpouring of the self, a bleeding of the self. Prayer is a form of bleeding of the ground of our being. Once we can see this then we will see that prayer is connected with who we really are. The essential nature of prayer is bound up with the whole self, it is indeed the language of this whole self. Thus it is not something imposed or artificial or "learned" as if this learning had to be acquired from outside the self. Indeed it has to be learned in the sense that it has to be practised and kept alive by daily activity. The best and most fruitful ways of keeping this "language of the self" alive have to be learned in the hard school of religion, but the language itself is not something foreign to the human person. It is not a question of learning Latin when your mother tongue is English or Spanish. Prayer is the mother tongue of the human person, it has simply been forgotten, dropped out of use because the languages we speak are regarded as more useful.

This then is the answer, or at least the beginnings of an answer, to the question thrust at us by the contemporary age about human nature. The contemporary age assumes that prayer is somehow unnatural, something that only religious people do (and then badly, so they are hypocrites) but which "normal" people do not need. Normality is not to pray. The reverse is actually the case. One way of making the case that normality is to pray would be to look at the human race from the point of view of a religious anthropologist and to show how in each culture and in each age human beings have invented means of prayer without prompting, as if this was a primary urge of the human spirit. This could be done, and indeed part of the new wave of European philosophy known as structuralism is more ready to be sympathetic to this approach because it sees the human pheonomenon in terms of patterns of behaviour which must be taken seriously in their own right rather than interpreted through the spectacles of European philosophy. I don't actually think there is very much wrong with this way of coming at the problem, but I think it is more immediately effective to look at the human person rather than at the human race and to find within the human person the language of prayer. This language may well be buried deep beneath the layers of consciousness that we possess, alienated by our acceptance of the predominant culture, we might even say "betrayed" by our accession to materialism, but it is there nevertheless.

". . . then I know that I must strike out and swim"

This is the approach which effectively Thomas
Merton pioneered and which has been followed in
recent years by a number of his disciples, notably John
Eudes, Henri Nouwen and, more recently still, by
Ann and Barry Ulanov.[5] The work of Ann and Barry
Ulanov is particularly interesting. They see prayer as
"primary speech", as the basic language of the human
person. As they see it, we all speak many languages.
These languages are not just verbal and linguistic such
as English, French or Kiswahili. Words with meanings
are only a very small section of the means of communication we use. Indeed there is an increasing body of
linguistic and philosophical opinion which would seriously question the view that there are words to which
we then attach "meanings" as if these meanings were
distinct entities which we can perceive separately and
then attach to or detach from words at will. But that
apart – at least for the moment! – the means by which
we communicate are not simply verbal. Language is
not simply a matter of words. There are also the spaces
between words, which may be long or short, empty or
anticipatory, full of meaning or ambiguity. Those
spaces are one of our languages. There are the different
tones in which the same words or set of words are
used to convey different meanings. There are the facial
expressions which then alter the meaning even further.
The language of our body conveys as much meaning
as the language of our words.

Prayer, the Ulanovs would say, is another of the
languages we speak, and in that sense is part of the
human repertoire, part of the way we are as human
beings. It is not a foreign imposition, a dead language

we have to learn but which nobody speaks any more. It is one of the many parts of speech which go to make up the human person. But they go on to say that there is also a special sense in which prayer is not just one of the languages we speak, it is also *the* language. Prayer is that language by which we as human beings offer and assert our own selves. It is the language by which we are totally open to who we are and with which we offer who we are to who it is that God is. It is, as it were, the basic language of honesty about ourselves. All of us pray, sometimes what we do we actually call prayer, but just as often what we are doing is prayer but is not called such and does not even appear to be worthy of the name of prayer. All of us pray when we engage in an activity which requires that we own or recognize the very ground of our being. We pray when we ask, plead, search, yearn for what we do not know out of what we know. We pray when the true self calls out in truth to him who gave that self a name at the beginning of things.

"To pray is to listen to and hear this self who is speaking. This speech is primary because it is basic and fundamental, our ground. In prayer we say who in fact we are – not who we should be, nor who we wish we were, but who we are. All prayer begins with this confession. Prayer is primary because this speech of confession comes first in any act of praying, whether we know it or not. In prayer we speak out of our "flesh", the ground of all our experience, collecting into awareness what our self is saying, both what we know and what we do not know . . ."[6]

Understanding prayer in this way is an important step forward. My point is that this self, this ground, is

142

in fact alienated, caught in a web of illusion and lies, under the sway of what we call "materialism", and that this is so to such an extent that this original self is unknown and, to a very large extent, feared. We do not want to allow this true self to emerge because we know, however dimly, that it would cause the utmost disruption in our lives. We would have to re-order our existence to a whole set of other criteria which are, at present, totally foreign to the way we live. The true self is, therefore, feared and repressed, called dark or black, endowed with negative force and denied. We do not pray because we live under the domination of a false self.

* * *

"Well", I thought, "that's much easier said than done. However do we arrive at such an understanding? What is it that will free us into seeing prayer in this way?"

I still think that there is a conceptual battle to be won. The way in which we conceive of and talk about prayer has to change. We have to shift our conceptual models from seeing prayer as an act of the will to seeing it as an act of attention. We have to move from seeing prayer as primarily concerned with asking to being something to do with adoration, with being before God, with standing, as Theophan says, "with the mind in the heart before the face of the living God". We have to undergo a conceptual shift in which we move from seeing prayer as something which we do, to seeing it as something which is done in us and into which we enter. Perhaps we even, at this point, have to listen to the charismatics, who talk about prayer in terms of "release", and who experience the flood of release from within as the ground of their being assumes more and more importance in their lives.

But as I reflected I knew that the battle for a new understanding was not simply a conceptual one. It has to be fought at the conceptual level, but in the end something has to happen which enables people to come to contemplative prayer, for that is what in the end we are talking about, from within. Something has to happen which gives people the courage to launch into the deep, to let go and start swimming in the ground of their being as Merton has to do in his dream. In the dream Merton wants to cross to the other side to join the party to which he is invited. He tries to go in a fishing boat, but cannot. So he decides to strike out and swim. This is the turning point, for he then finds himself absolutely carried and given great strength and vitality by the "beautiful magic water of the bay". The water gives him a life and power to which he knows he is not entitled but which he both loves and fears. This is an image of the life of grace, the life of the ground of his being. It swells up unasked from below. He knows that it is good but that he has to accept it as gift, not to swim down and investigate or appropriate it. He has to let it carry him.

This powerful passage is symbolic of the life of God which carries each one of us within. The water is the ground of our being which gives us identity and life and which carries us to our destination. This life of grace, which carries our prayer, which in the end is our prayer, is the key to our journey. To make it to the other side we have to strike out and swim. This is the difficult moment and I spent some time reflecting on how it might happen to us, how it might come about that we eventually let go.

And I remembered various people. I remembered the parishioner who said that she had abandoned intercession – "I can't do it", she said, "so I won't be a hypocrite and ask for anything. God knows everything anyway. He knows what I'm going to ask for and whether he's going to give it, so why ask?" thus revealing what a tight-fisted and predictable old god she believed in. Certainly not somebody who was always making everything new! Then she found herself drawn into a "Julian Group", a small cell of people who met regularly for silent prayer. And after a while she said, "Well, it's all a bit of a surprise. I started by being silent, doing the exercises as we were told, breathing and all the rest, but then I found that intercessory prayer came back to me. It took time, and I certainly wasn't expecting it or working towards it, but that is what happened. I found myself free again to pray for others, and I did. It comes out." I must admit to paraphrasing but that, if my memory serves, is the gist of what happened to her. To use Merton's language, she was swimming. To talk in the language of the Ulanovs she had discovered primary speech. It was provoked or set free in her by silence.

And then I remembered various students. In particular I remember one who came frequently to prayers in the little chapel we had furnished in the church, but she was busy, clinging, unsure but not wanting to be. And then her father died and her life was, for a while, shattered. In the end she left the practice of formal religion, graduated in law, and married an African who was deeply involved in the struggle for the freedom of his people. She now practises law and in particular defends those whom society rejects. She has great strength and enjoys, at great depth, who she is and what she does. Even though, for her, God is not formally involved, I believe she is swimming in the ground of her being. She has discovered who she is and allows it to come to her as gift. In a real sense her life *is* prayer, although she will not bless me for seeing it that way, for she sees her life as protest. She was set free, I believe, by the need to protest her father's death. Certainly she has discovered primary speech in a way which many who are locked into the business of the Church will never do.

In each case the people I remembered came to a shift of understanding by virtue of a crisis. Something happened which forced them to abandon their standard ways of prayer – a death, a desperation, a family crisis of some kind. All found themselves moving into a simpler, deeper, more "empty" way of praying when circumstances forced them to acknowledge that the standard ways were not enough. Several other things also happened at this point. For many people, and certainly this was true for my friend the law student, this discovery of an inner ground set them free to move towards others in a way which they had not been able to do before. Acceptance of grace within enabled confidence and service of others to emerge with great clarity and strength. Still others, who had been timid and withdrawn, found themselves able to share where they had not been able to share before. But in every case all this came, I thought, from an awareness of what can only be described as "Presence" or "Gift". This sense of "Presence" or "Life as a Gift" stills heart and mind, calms the chattering consciousness, releases inner silence and strength and enables compassion to flow.

After a while I began to gather some of these thoughts together and to try to put them into some semblance of order. This was an important experience because it gave me greater confidence that what I was beginning to think about the spiritual life had some coherence and pattern, and this confidence grew by leaps and bounds when I began to see that what I experienced myself and observed in others bore real relationship to the experience of others, that is the fathers of the Church both past and present. What I found was this.

When we open ourselves to the ground of our being this is an opening not just to the ground of the self but also to God. In that self-opening we discover He who is. The name of He who is is love. What we discover to be the ground of our being is not an emptiness but the darkness of love. In this darkness a number of things will happen. In the first place we will find ourselves assailed by demons. These demons are various and manifold. Some come from our past, from old hidden, unresolved conflicts and resentments linked to our childhood and upbringing. Some are jealousies and hurts linked to the way in which our life has developed. Some are connected to our present, the pattern of relationships we are involved in now, whereas others relate to the future and our fear of the unknown. In the silence of prayer all of these demons will come to assail us. They will emerge from the depths of our consciousness once the surface activity of our lives has been taken away. In the silence of prayer we will have to struggle with them and, in the confidence that the darkness is in truth the darkness of love, learn how to disarm them. This disarming does not occur by ignoring or suppressing our awareness of the presence of these demons. They have to be tackled and disarmed otherwise they return with greater force and in greater numbers to defeat us.

We have to learn from them what it is they can teach us about ourselves, what it is we lack, who it is that we have to forgive, what it is that we have to cease to fear. The demons we struggle with are, as much as anything, signs of our need. They are disarmed when we accept them as such. They are only demonic while we allow them to have power over us. What we have to learn from them above all is what it is that we fear most because it is in that fear that we are imprisoned and until we know what it is we cannot be set free. It may be that we are afraid of death or loss. It may be that we are imprisoned by the fear of being made to look foolish, and there is some truth in the sentiment that most of us are imprisoned in respectability, particularly the English. It may be that we are imprisoned in the need always to put our sense of grievance into circulation wherever we are, in some way poisoning the normal commerce of human intercourse with malice or innuendo of some kind. We can learn what it is we fear most and so begin to free ourselves of the captivity which this fear brings within the silence of prayer and the darkness of love with which prayer is surrounded. We have to speak ourselves into this silence and have our self given back to us forgiven, burned of dross. We then begin to know what it is of ourselves that we need and what it is, in the face of such overwhelming love, that we simply do not need.

But that is not all. The darkness of love is not only a place where we will be assailed by demons, it is also the place where we will experience absence, above all the absence of God. This is because in the end God is God and all metaphors drop away before his face; but also because what we know and cling to has to drop away, or even be stripped away from us. As Thomas Merton remarks,[7] we wrap ourselves in bandages in order to be seen by others and are unable to allow ourselves to exist without these protective layers of identity. In the silence of prayer and the darkness of love we will inevitably pass through a dark night of the soul. We will always carry this sense of unknowing with us on our journey. We have to come face to face with the absence of God. There are various refuges, some of them apparently religious. There is the superficial verbosity of some prayer groups who think that by continually talking to God they are in touch with him. There are the endless words of church committees, the continual practice of works of charity, the superfluity of retreats. Above all else there is the continuous chatter of our own self-consciousness. All of these refuges have to be shunned – they may be inhabited, we may stay with them, but we have to know that they are not where we have to go. In the end, if we are fortunate, we will come to a point where there is a wilderness, an emptiness and no way forward. Here we have to trust and allow ourselves to be found in God and to be content with that. We have to allow the bandages we have wrapped around ourselves to fall away in the joy of our resurrection.

This is the point at which a very great deal happens. We become "found". God speaks in us. His word is uttered in us and then we are free. We are not only free of illusions about ourselves and able to see ourselves clearly, but we are also free to see the world in which we live. We see its beauty. We see its singularity. We see its sheer gifted loveliness as it is. In fact we are able to see all things as they are. We see our stupidity and weep over it. We see our own strengths and are thankful for them. We see others as they are, both lovable and unlovable, but we love and enjoy them as they are.

That was what I found within my own experience. It's always difficult to let yourself pray and corroboration that you are on the right lines does become important, however much you think it ought not to be! The comforting thing was that I found others describing their experience in not too dissimilar terms. One of them, I found, is Edward Schillebeeckx. He employs the word "mystical" and divides this mystical path into three phases. Whether "mysticism" is the right word for my experience I doubt, but I certainly found myself recognizing his three phases. The first of these is the discovery of this experience as a totally new way of seeing which embraces all things. This is not too far away from the experience of Admiral Byrd discussed in chapter three. Schillebeeckx says, "Mystical experience is a source experience. Among mystics there is an awareness that something fundamental has happened, a sort of sense of enlightenment . . . There is something transcendent and at the same time all-embracing . . . an experience of totality, of reconciliation with all things." This is followed by a second stage which involves doubt and struggle together with an experience of absence. He says, "The second phase usually ends up in a night and a wilderness; authentic mysticism is often not fine, but a torment." But then there is the all-important third phase where the mystic's sense of the presence of the divine is imprinted into his being. The sense of loss is always present as well but this is now acceptable because the sense of presence is an overwhelming and all-embracing reality. "In the end mystics discover the features of the countenance of the divine Love, albeit only in the trace that the beloved has left . . ."[8]

Schillebeeckx uses the word "mystic". The difficulty with this is that it tends to imply that such an experience of prayer is open only to a few while the rest of us toil here below. Increasingly I am convinced that this is not the case and that what is often described as "mystical" is commonplace and that what we had thought was limited to a few is far more generalized. This path is a common possession. But the all-important thing about this way of prayer – the contemplative path as I would prefer to call it – is that it is liberating. It sets the person free to be who he or she really is. A free space is discovered within the self, a total freedom to accept or reject all of the powers of the age, a total realism about who we are, a total capacity to delight in creation and a total freedom to stand with those who are powerless.

It is in prayer that total freedom to support the powerless is discovered and released. We do not pray *so that* this will happen, we pray because we wish to stand before God in our own simplicity. Nor do we always know who it is that we shall be set free for. It may be that we think we should be set free for those who, at least from where we stand, are poor and despised, but we find ourselves being given to those with whom we can be genuinely free but who are, in fact, quite other than we expected or wanted. What is true is that the Church's bias to the poor requires contemplative prayer otherwise it degenerates into being mere politics. "Faith in the City" requires a spirituality so that it may avoid being caught up in mere social progress. But by the same argument politics requires contemplative prayer otherwise it loses its humanity, its capacity to discern where its action is truly needed and its strength to persevere in compassion even in the dark.

10

Remembering

When we wake from a dream it often takes a minute or so before we sense that we have returned to reality. There is usually a long moment when we are not quite sure where we are, asleep or awake, dreaming or conscious. Sometimes at this point we remember our dream and might spend some moments thinking about it, trying, perhaps, to relate it to our normal experience. In the end, however, we always come to absolutely and put aside the world of dreams and concentrate on the reality to hand. We get up, dress, go to work, deal with real life. The dream was only a dream after all.

Our everyday conviction is that life is reality and that dreams are dreams. However this distinction masks a number of truths. It masks the well-known truth that dreams can often help us to know more about ourselves. They can show us something of the reality we need to know about but which is, perhaps, hidden from us. More importantly the distinction masks the truth that the reality we think we inhabit may not be as real as we imagine. We may be living with a number of very real illusions about ourselves and our place within the world. We may behave in ways which are the consequence of these illusions. We may be alienated from the true nature of ourselves and where we really belong. The religious conviction, certainly the Christian one, is that this is almost always the case. We are actually asleep and need to wake up to reality, to turn and believe.

Plato's famous passage, where he depicts us chained inside a cave watching shadows on the wall and believing that they are reality, portrays this very clearly. In the Gospels Christ comes to call us into the light. Like Plato's prisoners we have to turn, lose our chains and stumble out of the dream into the reality of God. This is the journey we have to make and which is hidden from us because we have opted for a comfortable life of illusion. It is also hidden because it is a journey in the darkness. It is a journey in trust. It is also hidden in every part of our lives, in our work, in our wealth, in our loneliness. It is hidden in our religion, in prayer and in the eucharist. In each part of our lives we have to turn away from illusion and come to the true light. We have to wake from sleep. At every turn of the road we have to set out again and find the Christ – the first of many sisters and brothers, who has made the journey before us – place ourselves in his care and go out with him into God. The silence of prayer is the central place where, as we gently push our distractions away, we can lose our illusions and be able to rise, remembering that he has called us out of darkness into his own glorious light.

NOTES

CHAPTER 1

1. See *Primary Speech: A Psychology of Prayer* by Ann and Barry Ulanov (SCM Press, 1985).
2. *Conjectures of a Guilty Bystander* by Thomas Merton (Sheldon Press, 1977) p.29.

CHAPTER 3

1. *A Year Lost and Found* by Michael Mayne (Darton, Longman and Todd, 1987) p.73.
2. From "The Prelude" by William Wordsworth.
3. From "Folk Tale" in *Experimenting with An Amen* by R. S. Thomas (Macmillan, 1986).
4. *The Social God* by Kenneth Leech (Sheldon Press, 1981) p.80.
5. *The School of Genius* by Anthony Storr (André Deutsch, 1988) p.28.
6. From "A Letter on the Contemplative Life" in *The Monastic Journey* by Thomas Merton (Sheldon Press, 1977) p.173.
7. *The Monastic Journey* p.155.
8. "Notes for a Philosophy of Solitude" in *The Power and Meaning of Love* by Thomas Merton (Sheldon Press, 1976) p.72.
9. A phrase of Merton's used as the title of his first volume of letters *The Hidden Ground of Love* edited by William H. Shannon (Farrar Straus Giroux, 1985).
10. *The Inner Journey of the Poet* by Kathleen Raine (George Allen and Unwin, 1982) p.36.

CHAPTER 4

1. *A Time of Gifts* by Patrick Leigh-Fermor (Penguin, 1979) p.20.
2. Genesis 2:19.
3. *Christianity Rediscovered – An Epistle from the Masai* by Vincent J. Donovan (SCM Press, 1982) p.91.
4. Quotations from *Conjectures of a Guilty Bystander* p.260ff.

CHAPTER 5

1. A distinction used by Henri Nouwen in *Reaching Out* (Fount, 1980).
2. Hosea 2:14.
3. "Is the World a Problem?" in *Contemplation in a World of Action* by Thomas Merton (Unwin, 1971) p.154.
4. *Jesus in our Western Culture* by Edward Schillebeeckx (SCM Press, 1987) p.69.

CHAPTER 6

1. *Reflections on the Beatitudes* by Simon Tugwell (Darton, Longman and Todd, 1980) p.22.
2. *Poems of St John of the Cross* translated by Roy Campbell (Fount, 1979) p.45.
3. *Cry the Gospel With Your Life* by The Little Brothers and Little Sisters of Jesus (Dimension Books, 1981) p.64.
4. *Letters from the Desert* by Carlo Carretto (Darton, Longman and Todd, 1972) p.75.

CHAPTER 7

1. *Christian Ministry and Further Education*: *The Report of a Project, 1982–5* by Edwina Sherrington (available from Bristol Diocesan Office, 23 Great George Street, Bristol).

2. Reprinted in *Proclaiming Justice and Peace* edited by Michael Walsh and Brian Davies (CAFOD/Collins, 1984) p.310.
3. Quotations from *Conjectures of a Guilty Bystander* p.78ff.

CHAPTER 8

1. *Collected Poems 1935–1980* by Kathleen Raine (George Allen and Unwin, 1981) p.33.

CHAPTER 9

1. On this question of "uselessness" in prayer, see especially *Does God Answer Prayer* by Peter Baelz (Darton, Longman and Todd, 1982).
2. See *The Shadow of the Galilean* by Gerd Theissen (SCM Press, 1987).
3. See *Delighting in God* by Melvyn Matthews (Fount, 1987).
4. *And Your Deserts Shall Flower* by Brother Roger of Taizé (Mowbray, 1984).
5. *Primary Speech* by Ann and Barry Ulanov (SCM Press, 1985).
6. *Primary Speech* p.1.
7. *Seeds of Contemplation* by Thomas Merton (Anthony Clarke Books, 1972) p.27.
8. *Jesus in our Western Culture* p.68ff.

Also available in Fount Paperbacks

BOOKS BY C. S. LEWIS

Christian Reflections

'This collection . . . deserves the warmest of Christian welcomes on this happy reappearance . . . a devastating counter-attack on the "new morality" and a magnificent restatement of the essence of the Gospel and the faith.'

Church Times

The Four Loves

'He has never written better. Nearly every page scintillates with observations which are illuminating, provocative and original.'

Church Times

Prayer: Letters to Malcolm

'A book full of wisdom, of bitter honesty and of deep charity. It nowhere tells us "how to pray" but . . . stimulates afresh that hunger and thirst for God without which we should never pray at all.'

J. B. Phillips

The Pilgrim's Regress

'A welcome reappearance in paperback. Bunyanesque in form, as the title suggests, this reissue may well pick up a new generation of readers . . .'

Methodist Recorder

Fount Paperbacks

Fount is one of the leading paperback publishers of religious books and below are some of its recent titles.

- [ ] FRIENDSHIP WITH GOD David Hope £2.95
- [ ] THE DARK FACE OF REALITY Martin Israel £2.95
- [ ] LIVING WITH CONTRADICTION Esther de Waal £2.95
- [ ] FROM EAST TO WEST Brigid Marlin £3.95
- [ ] GUIDE TO THE HERE AND HEREAFTER
       Lionel Blue/Jonathan Magonet £4.50
- [ ] CHRISTIAN ENGLAND (1 Vol) David Edwards £10.95
- [ ] MASTERING SADHANA Carlos Valles £3.95
- [ ] THE GREAT GOD ROBBERY George Carey £2.95
- [ ] CALLED TO ACTION Fran Beckett £2.95
- [ ] TENSIONS Harry Williams £2.50
- [ ] CONVERSION Malcolm Muggeridge £2.95
- [ ] INVISIBLE NETWORK Frank Wright £2.95
- [ ] THE DANCE OF LOVE Stephen Verney £3.95
- [ ] THANK YOU, PADRE Joan Clifford £2.50
- [ ] LIGHT AND LIFE Grazyna Sikorska £2.95
- [ ] CELEBRATION Margaret Spufford £2.95
- [ ] GOODNIGHT LORD Georgette Butcher £2.95
- [ ] GROWING OLDER Una Kroll £2.95

All Fount Paperbacks are available at your bookshop or newsagent, or they can be ordered by post from Fount Paperbacks, Cash Sales Department, G.P.O. Box 29, Douglas, Isle of Man. Please send purchase price plus 22p per book, maximum postage £3. Customers outside the UK send purchase price, plus 22p per book. Cheque, postal order or money order. No currency.

NAME (Block letters) _____

ADDRESS_____

_____

_____